100
TEXAS WILDFLOWERS

D1470064

Dorothy Baird Mattiza
for the
Native Plant Society of Texas

WESTERN NATIONAL PARKS ASSOCIATION
TUCSON, ARIZONA

The net proceeds from WNPA publications support educational and
research programs in the national parks. Receive a free Western
National Parks Association catalog, featuring hundreds of publications. Email: info@wnpa.org or visit www.wnpa.org

Published in association with the Native Plant Society of Texas.
Editorial: Ron Foreman
Design: Campana Design
Map: Crane Design
Cover photograph: Texas bluebonnet, *Lupinus texensis* Hook,
    Indian paintbrush, *Castilleja* sp. Gray, and other wildflowers,
    by Laurence Parent.
Printed in China by C&C Offset Printing

ABOUT TEXAS

*W*hen you travel the breadth of Texas, you realize that the state is vast and dramatically diverse. In the 773 miles from east to west, the average annual rainfall decreases 51.4 inches, from 59.2 inches at Orange, to 7.8 inches at El Paso—an average of one inch every fifteen miles. Surprisingly, more than half of the plant species in this book are adapted to both arid and wet extremes, and to the wide range and wild fluctuations of temperatures, from the far northwest corner of the state to the southeast tip, eight hundred miles away.

The diversity of Texas is not due to size alone. The state's continental location straddles the hundredth meridian, in a "melting pot" of the plant and animal world where east blends with west. As rainfall decreases, the tall grasses of the Grand Prairies blend into mixed, or mid-grass, prairie and finally become the short grasses of the Great Plains. All extend from Canada through the central United States to their southern limits at the Balcones Escarpment, in south-central Texas. In a broad swath between the southern part of this scarp and the Rio Grande River, tropical species inch northward, only to freeze back in harsh winters. North meets south.

Texas has the most extensive collection of the adaptable flora and fauna of the North American continent. Extreme weather patterns and geologic formations combine to form a wonderfully varied topography with distinct vegetation regions. Some genetically adaptable species have narrowed their range to become quite site-specific within these regions. In isolated niches, some have evolved as separate species found nowhere else. Texas provides habitat for more than five thousand flowering plants.

A quarter-million miles of roads crisscross plateaus, rivers, springs, streams, arroyos, canyons, floodplains, meadows, prairies, deserts, mountains, hills, valleys, deltas, resacas, bayous, and beaches in Texas. From the roads, clues to the geologic evolution responsible for the mixed topography and soil types can often be seen.

YOUR GUIDE TO TEXAS FLORA

*W*ith each plant pictured in this book, the numbers of the vegetation regions where it can be found are listed. Cities and towns located on the map will help orient you. Plants are organized by color. If you find a yellow flower in the Dallas area, look in the yellow-flower section and check for flowers that are in Region 4, where Dallas is situated. If you don't find the specimen, the text may help determine if it is closely related to a flower pictured. Closely related species often hybridize, making identification difficult.

Edith Bettinger

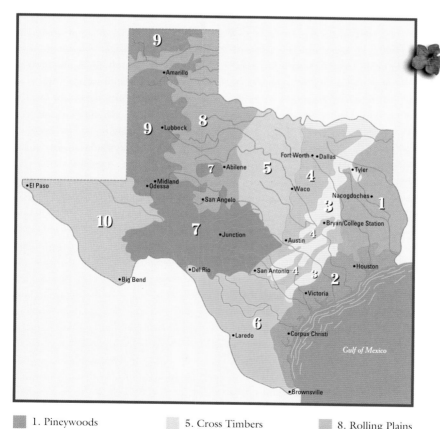

1. Pineywoods
2. Gulf Prairies & Marshes
3. Post-Oak Savannah
4. Blackland Prairies
5. Cross Timbers & Prairies
6. South Texas Plains
7. Edwards Plateau
8. Rolling Plains
9. High Plains
10. Trans-Pecos

REGIONS OF TEXAS

So diverse is the flora of Texas that a map has been developed to guide botanists and others through ten major vegetation regions. Notice the map on the opposite page. Knowing a little about each region will help you locate plants and understand a little more about the natural history of Texas.

REGION 1: PINEYWOODS

The land is gently rolling and partly forested in the Pineywoods region. This is part of the much larger pine-hardwood forest that extends from Louisiana, Arkansas, and eastern Oklahoma, and south and west into Texas. Its boundaries are determined by acidic, sandy, or sandy loam soils, and by the evenly distributed annual rainfall, which averages fifty-six inches, decreasing to an average of forty inches at its southern and western limits. Elevations range from two hundred to five hundred feet. The region's size, approximately 24,700 square miles, is larger than New Hampshire, Vermont, and Connecticut combined. Swamps are common, humidity is high, temperatures are warm and mild, and breezes are welcome. Persistent winds are absent. Alligators, white-tailed deer, river otters, flying squirrels, foxes, raccoons, opossums, muskrat, beavers, and swamp rabbits all live here, and the red-cockaded woodpecker survives in remaining old-stand pine forests. The wetlands support many species of waterfowl. Birds and butterflies abound; there are fireflies and magnolias; and accents are thick. In the Pineywoods, the Deep South touches Texas.

REGION 2: GULF PRAIRIES AND MARSHES

The slowly draining coastal plain rises to a maximum of only 250 feet above sea level. This nearly level area is approximately twenty-five thousand square miles. Barrier islands protect 350 miles of coastline and saline marshes that are extremely productive estuaries. The warm, humid climate is punctuated with hurricanes, strong winds, and storms. Shade is sparse, but the long growing season provides food for local wildlife, the additional seasonal residents, and the migrants. Rainfall, fairly evenly distributed throughout the year, decreases from fifty to twenty inches, north to south. Marsh soils generally are dark sandy loam or clay, acidic in the north, more neutral in the south. River bottoms and deltas are composed of loamy to dark, clayey alluvial soils. There are areas of wind-blown sands and dunes in a narrow inland strip along the coast. Overgrazed original vegetation of tall prairie grasses and post-oak savannah is now replaced by invasive species such as acacias, honey mesquite, and prickly pear. The endangered Attwater's prairie chicken is found in small pockets of remaining grasslands. On a major flyway for migrating birds, the region is world-famous for its bird-watching opportunities. More than four hundred species have been recorded at Rockport. Less noticeable is the flora supporting the avian richness. "Watching the grass grow" may become just as important as watching the birds.

REGION 3: POST-OAK SAVANNAH

Just west of the Pineywoods, the rolling wooded plain is approximately twenty thousand square miles, and ranges in elevation from three hundred to eight hundred feet. Rainfall becomes seasonal here, peaking in May or June. Annual averages decrease from forty-five inches, north and east, to thirty-five inches, south and west. Light-colored upland soils are generally droughty, slightly acidic, sandy loam or sands over a claypan that restricts moisture percolation. Alluvial bottomland soils that support hardwoods and shrubs are acid to calcareous (limy). There are peat bogs, some marshy areas, and notable intrusions of the Blackland Prairies in this region. Oaks occur in association with the tall grasses on the plains. Some white-tailed deer and turkeys are found here, with squirrels, rabbits, other small forms of wildlife, and many species of birds.

REGION 4: BLACKLAND PRAIRIES

Further west, weather patterns change. Heaviest rainfall occurs in May, with a second peak in September. The Blackland Prairies have annual rainfall that varies from forty-five inches in the northeast to thirty inches in the southwest. This more than twenty-five thousand square-mile area is well drained. Upland soils are dark-colored clays, locally called "black gumbo." There are also some gray, acidic, sandy loams. Isolated areas of these same soil types can be found in Region 3. Once a mid-grass prairie, this land became very productive agriculturally in the late nineteenth century. Ninety-five percent of it was plowed, leaving few remnants of prairie. This was the southern extension of the Grand Prairie, stretching from Canada to Texas, that became known as the breadbasket of America. In this region, many eastern birds reach their western limits.

REGION 5: CROSS TIMBERS AND PRAIRIES

Variable and diverse topography characterizes this region of nearly twenty-four thousand square miles. Oak and hickory typify the Cross Timbers vegetation, and the Grand Prairie supports the tall- and mid-grasses. The terrain has an elevation of five hundred to fifteen hundred feet. Rainfall varies from an average of thirty-five inches in the northeast to twenty-five inches in the west and south. As in Region 4, May is the month of highest rainfall, followed by a second peak in September. Upland soils of both the East and West Cross

Timbers are slightly acidic sands or sandy loam, but neutral to calcareous (limy) clays and loamy alluvial soils are in river valleys, which support many hardwoods such as hackberry, pecan, elm, and oak. Shaley ridges, found in prairie areas, are mixed with rapidly draining sandstone. Wildflowers seem to thrive, making springtime a special treat, although there is some invasion by junipers, mesquite, scrub, and live oak from past grazing practices. Jackrabbits, ringtails (a cat-sized carnivore), gray foxes, and badger are found in the region.

REGION 6: SOUTH TEXAS PLAINS

Nearly the size of Maine, the level to rolling South Texas Plains consist of more than 32,600 square miles. Soil types are mixed, from deep sand to clay or loam, and range from saline to limy. The rate of evaporation is very high, and droughts are common. Rainfall, lowest in January and February, annually averages from thirty inches in the east to only eighteen in the west. Elevations increase gradually from sea level to one thousand feet. Originally, grasslands along the coast were punctuated with treed savannahs, and the mixed brush-land to the west had ridges frequently capped with dense thickets. Oak, pecan, mesquite, and hackberry grew along streams, but from early historical times this land was grazed heavily, giving the woody species ample opportunity to increase. South Texas is now almost all brush country, although most of it is still pastured. The area is famous for its large ranches, including the well-known King Ranch. South Texas abounds with game, supporting more species of wildlife than any other region. The white-tailed deer are noted for their large size. Javelina, white-winged dove, quail, and turkeys are abundant. In the fertile Rio Grande Valley, little is left of the original tropical vegetation because of severe cropping. Major conservation efforts have been initiated to buy valley land on which to preserve or reintroduce native flora and habitat, an ecosystem where tropical deciduous forests, plants, and many birds and animals reach their northern limit.

REGION 7: EDWARDS PLATEAU

The Edwards Plateau encompasses nearly forty thousand square miles (almost as large as Virginia), and the eastern and southern boundaries are easily recognized. Most early explorers and settlers entered Texas from lower country, the plains of the south and east. They saw the escarpment rising before them as hills. In reality, the "Hill Country" they saw was the eroded edge of the huge Edwards Plateau, uplifted when shifting continental plates gave rise to the Rocky Mountains and lowered the silted lands to the south and east of the Balcones Fault zone. Road cuts expose multi-layers of limestone containing fossils deposited in the beds of ancient seas. There are many flowing springs and seeps, and the area is deeply dissected by streams and rivers that drain rapidly in a southeasterly direction to the Gulf of Mexico. Another distinctive geologic feature of the Edwards Plateau is the Central Mineral region, dominated by Precambrian granite domes and outcrops. Its mineral-rich, gravelly soils nourish a profusion of wildflowers. The balance of the Edwards Plateau is a flat to undulating, broad, stony plain of shallow soil that rises from about six hundred feet in the southeast to three thousand feet in the northwest. Plateau rainfall averages from thirty-two inches in the east to a xeric twelve inches in the southwest. The grassland-savannah-type landscape was grazed until it was too barren to support cattle, and the economy shifted to goats. As a result, brush and ash juniper, once restricted to rocky slopes and streamsides, now invade the entire plateau. Explosive increases in the deer population, resulting from the eradication of the screwworm, and introduction of exotic game for hunting are further threatening the diversity of forb (wildflower) species essential to all forms of local wildlife. Popularity of the "Hill Country" for recreation and retirement continues to fragment the land and reduce habitat, crowding wildlife into ever-decreasing space to compete for available food and water. Too often, the pressure on available vegetation restricts many wildflowers to a strip of land between roads and fences, or to bluffs where they are not within reach of feeding animals.

REGION 8: ROLLING PLAINS

Located between the Cross Timbers and the High Plains, this nearly level-to-rolling land is also a part of the Great Plains of the central United States. Rising from one thousand to three thousand feet, it is arid, with annual rainfall averaging twenty-five inches in the east, decreasing to eighteen inches in the west. Its western edge abuts the caprock escarpment known as the Llano Estacado, and it pokes a finger through the northern High Plains, in the Canadian River Breaks. There is moderate to rapid surface drainage. Sandy loams or clay soils are neutral to chalky. Saline, shallow, and stony soils are common, and there are only minor amounts of good alluvial bottomlands. Although 75 percent of the area is still rangeland, short grasses, shrubs and annual forbs have replaced original tall- and mid-grasses of the prairie, a result of grazing. There is little farming in the region, but there is a good mix of food and habitat for the abundant wildlife.

REGION 9: HIGH PLAINS

The High Plains gradually rise, at a rate of only eight feet per mile, from three thousand feet in the south to forty-five hundred feet in the north. This windswept part of the Great Plains is relatively level, separated from the Rolling Plains on the east by the Llano Estacado. In addition to the cut made by the

Canadian River Breaks, the Prairie Dog Town Fork of the Red River gives relief to the flat plains. It has carved the spectacular thousand-foot-deep Palo Duro Canyon, leaving spires and pinnacles behind, as it continues its journey eastward to the Mississippi River. Further south, another beautiful gorge along the caprock, Tule Canyon, exposes more rock strata and knife-edged buttes. Distinct plant communities are found in all of these rugged draws and breaks. Rainfall averages fifteen to twenty-one inches. Playa lakes, shallow siltation depressions that fill with rainwater, have unique patterns of vegetation that support thousands of waterfowl seeking winter refuge, or that migrate through the continent's Central Flyway. Antelope, once common in this region, are now reduced to only remnant populations, but the region supports mule deer, badger, foxes, coyotes, turkeys, quail, mourning dove, and other wildlife.

REGION 10: TRANS-PECOS

It is hard *not* to be fascinated by the desert. A large part of the Trans-Pecos region is Chihuahuan desert. Sparse vegetation in this arid land often leaves the geologic record exposed. A prime example is a spectacular formation known as El Capitan, which rises to more than eight thousand feet in the Guadalupe Mountains, just south of the New Mexico border. This relic of prehistoric seas was once a limestone reef. The only true mountains in Texas are found in the Trans-Pecos, the southern extension of the Rocky Mountains. Rainfall and cooler temperatures in the higher elevations support ponderosa pine above the creosote-tarbush shrub of the desert floor, where mean daily maximum temperatures reach or exceed one hundred degrees for five months of the year. The dramatic Chisos Mountains in Big Bend National Park on the Rio Grande River are an ecological island in the desert sea. Extinct volcanoes, gypsum dunes, rugged canyons, and gorges are all topographical features that contribute to the tremendous diversity of habitat. Elevation changes influence the climate. Higher elevations receive maximum rainfall and have cooler temperatures, defining zones of distinct plant types. In climbing just a few hundred feet, you can pass through several markedly different ecosystems. Mule deer, pronghorn antelope, javelina, and mountain lions join many smaller wildlife species to find a home in the wilderness of the Trans-Pecos. More than 385 bird species have been recorded in Big Bend National Park.

THE PLEASURE OF PLANT WATCHING

Observing native plants, you may marvel at how they have managed to survive. Many have extraordinary adaptations, enabling them to thrive in a sometimes harsh environment. Hairs shade them, roots store food and water, and many plants "root cellar" for winter.

Some fold up their leaves on hot afternoons, spreading them to the sun the next morning. Bright colors, sweet scents, and lined pathways lure pollinators that help them reproduce. Barbs and spines defend them, and toxic chemicals repel grazing animals. Some plants throw their seed to the wind; others catch a ride on your socks, or perhaps in a bird's belly... to be planted in a fertilized pellet. Many seeds just drop to the ground and wait for rain, carrying chemical inhibitors to avoid germination unless conditions favor their sprouts.

Some knowledge of plant structure may increase your ability to identify plants and your pleasure in plant watching. Below is a sketch of the flower parts referred to in the text.

In the back of this book is a visual glossary with sketches of a few ways leaves and flowers are arranged on their stems, and a few of their common forms or shapes to aid you in recognizing terms with which you may not be familiar. We have also included a short glossary of definitions.

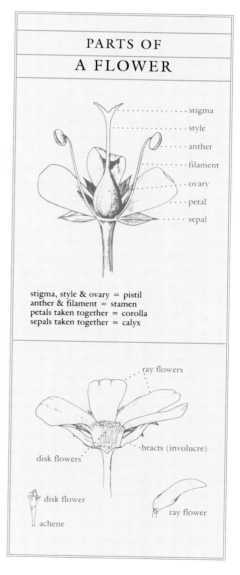

PARTS OF A FLOWER

stigma
style
anther
filament
ovary
petal
sepal

stigma, style & ovary = pistil
anther & filament = stamen
petals taken together = corolla
sepals taken together = calyx

ray flowers
disk flowers
bracts (involucre)
disk flower
ray flower
achene

PLANT NAMES

Most of our basic needs, including food, medicine, clothing, fuel, shelter, and dyes are supplied by plants. Daily contact with plants is critical to our survival, and it can be dangerous for one plant to be mistaken for another. Common names are too local and frequently differ from town to town. Several species of plants often carry the same common name. In order to communicate with accuracy, a universal way of naming both plants and animals was devised in 1753 by Carolus Linnaeus, a Swedish botanist. This binomial system of naming plants and animals consists of a noun, which is the generic name, or genus, followed by a specific name, the species. The species name is often an adjective, such as *alba*, as in *polygala alba*, describing this milkwort (generic name) specifically as white, *alba*. In *Cnidoscolus texanus*, Texas bullnettle is being described by its location. On occasion, the name is in honor of a person, such as *Sctellaria drummondii*, or Drummond skullcap, honoring a distinguished Scottish botanist, Thomas Drummond, who collected botanical and zoological specimens in Texas in 1833–1834. These names are always in Latin, the universal language at the time the system was invented. A species is a population enough alike to be considered all one kind.

In this text, the common name appears first, followed by the italicized Latin name then the authority who first described the species. We then give the common family name in capital letters, and the Latin family name in parentheses. You may be surprised to find how many of the Latin names you already know or find familiar because you recognize their Latin roots.

PLANT IDENTIFICATION

A range of sizes and flowering times is given for each plant. The great variability in climate and topography in Texas results in corresponding variability in plant size and flowering time. In Region 1, with deep soil and plentiful rainfall, an aster may be twice as large as the same plant growing on shale in the arid west. Bluebonnets in the south sometimes bloom and set seed six weeks before their northern sisters even begin to flower, so the bloom time noted means that you may expect to find that plant in flower somewhere in the state during that time. By understanding the local conditions, altitude, weather, and other habitat considerations, you can judge the probability that you have correctly identified a wildflower.

PLANT SELECTION

Deciding which one hundred wildflowers to include in this book was difficult. Plants that are so site-specific that they are unlikely to be seen along the roadside (such as columbines, which favor shady streamsides) were eliminated. We did not include cacti, vines, flowering woody shrubs, or trees. Naturalized plants, such as yarrow and mullein, and recent introductions, such as California poppy and red clover, were excluded.

The choices were narrowed further to plants seen in several vegetation regions. Regional additions were made from suggestions sent by members from twenty-four chapters of the Native Plant Society of Texas. A panel of members, botanists, and photographers determined the one hundred species finally chosen.

We hope you will enjoy meeting our choices as you travel through Texas, and that these flowers will whet your appetite for the sport of botanizing. Many of the flower species pictured are representative of their genus or family. You'll recognize their close cousins scattered across the state, often overlapping vegetation regions.

CONSERVATION

Enjoy the flowers. Smell them. Touch them. Study them. Understand them. But respect their vulnerability. Don't pick, dig, or cut plants. If you identify a flower you'd like to grow, try to locate it in a nursery that carries container-grown plants. With a full root system, these plants are far more likely to survive. *Do not buy plants dug from the wild.*

If you are a knowledgeable plant enthusiast, you might wish to collect a few ripe seeds to propagate. Collect from plants you can positively identify and then only if the seed crop is abundant. If you are in doubt, don't collect. It is against the law to collect seed of endangered or threatened plants, and it is your responsibility to know them. In the past, collection from the wild by the commercial trade and hobbyists contributed to an alarming loss of rare plants. It is up to each of us to protect and preserve what remains.

Larry Ulrich

NATIVE PLANTS FOR LANDSCAPING

For information on where you can buy seed or container-grown native plants, contact:

NATIVE PLANT SOCIETY OF TEXAS
P.O. Box 891, Georgetown, TX 78627
(512) 863-9685

NATIONAL WILDFLOWER RESEARCH CENTER
2600 FM 973 North, Austin, TX 78725-4201
(512) 929-3600

Laurence Parent

1 · Texas Bullnettle Mala Mujer

RANGE	1, 2, 3, 4, 5, 6, 7, 8, 10
SIZE	1–3 1/2 feet
BLOOMS	Mar.–Sept., Perennial

Dorothy Baird Mattiza

Be very careful if you want to smell these flowers! Bullnettle is well defended, with stinging hairs covering all parts except the flowers. Once stung, you'll know this plant forever. Upright and branched, it is common across Texas and frequently forms large colonies in disturbed areas. Fragrant, white, tubular flowers consist of five to seven flaring sepals that form loose terminal clusters. Seeds are held tightly in compartments of a tough, almost round seedpod, and the large, edible seeds are considered very tasty when ripe. A deep, tuberous taproot, branching underground, lets bullnettle thrive during hot summers and drought. Mala mujer (bad woman), another common name, was given because, like a "bad woman," bullnettle is hurtful to touch.

Cnidoscolus texanus (Muell. Arg.) Small
Spurge Family (Euphorbiaceae)

2 · Barbara's Buttons

Vernon L. Wesby

No one knows how Barbara's buttons got its name, but there is no doubt that this dainty little flower attracts the eye. Most often it is white, but it may also be pale pink, creamy, or lavender. The flower head, topping a slender stem, is one and one-half inches across and is composed of numerous fragrant disk flowers that form a lacy-looking ball. Stems may be solitary, or several, forming a clump. There are two varieties of this plant. *M. caespitosa var. caespitosa* has slender leaves, six inches long, crowded near the base, with bare stems supporting the flower heads. *M. caespitosa var. signata* has leafy stems and is endemic to south and midwest Texas, where it sometimes forms colonies.

Marshallia caespitosa DC.
Sunflower Family (Asteraceae)

RANGE	Range: 1, 2, 3, 4, 5, 6, 7, 8
SIZE	6–8 inches
BLOOMS	Apr.–June, Perennial

3 · White Milkwort

Dorothy Baird Mattiza

RANGE	2, 3, 4, 5, 6, 7, 8, 9, 10
SIZE	8–16 inches
BLOOMS	Mar.–Oct., Perennial

Milkworts do not have the sticky white sap that oozes from milkweeds when they are cut, so don't let the similar names confuse you. White milkwort has many erect stems growing from a woody base. The tiny leaves are sparse. They alternate up a stem that ends in a spike-like raceme of densely clustered, quarter-inch white flowers. Certain species in this family were believed to increase the flow of milk when grazed by cows. The botanical name is from the Greek words *poly* (many) and *galu* (milk). The dried, powdered root is commercially marketed for the treatment of respiratory ailments. More than twenty-five species of milkwort are found in Texas.

Polygala alba Nutt
Milkwort Family (Polygalaceae)

4 · White Pricklepoppy

Pricklepoppy often colonizes several acres of abandoned fields or overgrazed land. Plants in this family, which include the opium poppy, are slightly poisonous. White pricklepoppy is easily recognized by its large, cup-shaped flowers with wrinkled petals. It is centered with a globe of numerous yellow or reddish stamens surrounding a purple stigma. Alternate leaves are stiff, stalkless, and bluish green, with conspicuous blue veins. They are deeply lobed and edged with spine-tipped teeth. The plant has yellow sap. Flowers and sap of related species vary in color. Flowers may be pale pink, white, lavender, or yellow, and the sap can be red, orange, yellow, or milky white. Although

Jean E. Hardy

avoided by livestock, pricklepoppy is very attractive to its insect pollinators. You can usually observe their feeding frenzy by taking a close look into the flower's center. Seeds of *Argemone* yield oil and are used for food. They can also be ground and applied to sores.

Argemone squarrosa Greene
Poppy Family (Papaveraceae)

RANGE	1, 2, 3, 4, 5, 6, 7
SIZE	3–4 feet
BLOOMS	Apr.–Oct., Annual/Biennial

5 · White Dogstooth-Violet

White dogstooth-violet is a small plant that forms extensive colonies, spreading from underground shoots. A bare stem produces a single flower that hangs over, with its petals curved back, skyward. The nodding flower seems too large for its slender stem. Its six petals are yellow on the inside but are white to a lovely pale violet on the outside. Leaves are three to eight inches long, tapering at both ends. They have thick blades and are mottled purple-brown or light green. A plant with one leaf is immature, but plants with two leaves are mature and will flower. It has been reported that Indian children relished the crunchy, mild-flavored bulbs in the early spring, but these have never been a major food source. White dogstooth-violet is found on rich, moist loams, along slopes, sometimes under brush, or in shaded areas.

Erythronium albidum Nutt.
Lily Family (Liliaceae)

Jeffery G. Schultz

RANGE	1, 3, 4, 5
SIZE	8–10 inches
BLOOMS	Feb.–May, Perennial

6 · Spiderlily

Snow-white spiderlily is easily recognized by the way the stamens are joined by a hymen (membrane), forming a cup. This cup is surrounded by six very narrow, "spidery" tepals, which may reach up to seven inches across. A leafless, two-edged stem supports two or three open blossoms and several buds. The shiny leaves that grow basally from a four- to five-inch bulb may reach thirty inches in length, yet are usually less than an inch wide. A distinctive member of the Amaryllis family, spiderlily is common along ditches, streams, and in marshy places in east Texas. The bulbs divide to form large colonies. Spiderlily is toxic.

Hymenocallis spp.
Amaryllis Family (Amaryllidaceae)

Jean E. Hardy

RANGE	1, 2, 3, 4
SIZE	3 feet
BLOOMS	Mar.–May, Perennial

7· Small Coast Germander

Vernon L. Wesby

Germander is represented in Texas by three species with several subspecies. Germander has square stems and opposite leaves. All species form colonies. Small coast germander (pictured) has lobed, cleft, or scalloped leaves. Stalked white flowers are three-fourths of an inch long. *T. laciniatum*, cutleaf germander, flowers in the leaf axils. It has half-inch white flowers, and the broadly lobed leaves are incised nearly to the midrib. *T. canadense*, American germander, or wood sage, has flower spikes up to eight inches long, with individual flowers reaching a length of one-half to three-quarters of an inch. They may be creamy white, pale pink, or pale lavender.

Teucrium cubense Jacq.
Mint Family (Labiatae)

RANGE	2, 3, 4, 6, 10
SIZE	2 feet
BLOOMS	Mar.–Dec., Annual/Perennial

8· Stickleaf

Stickleaf is appropriately named. Most species of *Mentzelia* have rough, hairy leaves, easily detached from the plant. Barbs of the hairs cause leaves to cling to clothing or animals and are not easily brushed off. Fragrant flowers, ranging in size from two to three inches across, are white, and they open in the late afternoon. They have ten petals (thus the name *decapetala*) and up to two hundred stamens. Stems are often white or ash-white. Another species, *M. oligosperma*, has five petals; its flowers open in the morning, withering with the afternoon heat. *Mentzelia* sprawls or reclines to form mats or clumps. The oily seeds of some species can be parched or roasted and eaten.

Vernon L. Wesby

Mentzelia decapetala (Sims) Urban & G.
Loasa Family (Loasaceae)

RANGE	4, 5, 8, 9
SIZE	4 feet
BLOOMS	June–Aug., Perennial

9 · Rainlily

Stems and leaves of rainlilies grow from a bulb, and each stem usually bears a single flower. White, heavy-textured, fragrant blossoms flare from a pinkish tube that varies in length according to the species. One of the most common species in Texas is *C. pedunculata*, which has a tube up to one and one-half inches long, its six petals spreading to two inches across. It blooms in the spring and early summer. *C. drummondii*, with a tube that may reach seven inches long and a relatively small flower head, is more widespread; it blooms from late summer through fall. The habit of appearing in grassy areas soon after rains, often in large numbers, gives rainlilies their name.

Cooperia drummondii Herb.
Amaryllis Family (Amarylliadaceae)

RANGE	1, 2, 4, 6, 7
SIZE	1–1 1/2 feet
BLOOMS	Apr.–Oct., Perennial

Harry T. Cliffe

10 · White Rock-Lettuce

White rock-lettuce is a small, smooth plant. Most of its leaves are at ground level, but a few advance up the stem. These are one to three inches long, and are usually sparingly lobed. Leaves and stems exude a milky sap when broken. Solitary flowers at the top of stems are white to yellowish above, pinkish to rose-lavender underneath. The flower heads are one or two inches across with many petals, which are square-toothed at their tips. White rock-lettuce is widespread and is found in many habitats, especially on dry gravelly or calcareous (limy) soils or rock outcrops. It has good ornamental qualities.

Pinaropappus roseus (Less.)
Sunflower Family (Asteraceae)

Jean E. Hardy

RANGE	2, 5, 6, 7, 8, 10
SIZE	6–18 inches
BLOOMS	Mar.–May, Perennial

11 · Antelope Horns

Robert & Linda Mitchell

RANGE	4, 5, 6, 7, 8
SIZE	1–2 feet
BLOOMS	Mar–Nov., Perennial

Antelope horns is a milkweed with stout, spreading stems. It forms a low clump one to two feet across. Chartreuse, star-shaped flowers are clustered at the end of the stems in three- to four-inch balls. Most leaves are opposite and sometimes are folded together along the mid-rib. Antelope horns thrives in a sunny location in well-drained sand or gravel. The plant provides an important food for butterfly larvae, but like almost all of the milkweeds, it is extremely poisonous to livestock. It has been used medicinally for several hundred years, however. The fluffy hairs attached to the plant's flat seeds, and exposed when the okra-shaped pods open, are used to insulate gloves and vests.

Asclepias asperula (Dene.) Woods
Milkweed Family (Asclepiadaceae)

12 · Rock-Trumpet, Flor de San Juan

For sheer drama, few plants surpass rock-trumpet. Although infrequently seen, it is a plant that you will want to know, should you stumble upon it. Usually pure white, but occasionally tinged with pink, the flowers of rock-trumpet have five propeller-like petals, on a slim, two- to five-inch-long tube. Opening in the evening, their sweet fragrance is said to attract moths from as far as three miles away. The fuzzy leaves are paired, ovate, elliptic, or almost round, and are on very short stalks. Stems are partly woody, and if broken exude a sticky, milky juice. Twin seedpods form a three-inch "V" shape. Rock-trumpet is found on open, rocky, or brushy slopes and road cuts, where it sometimes forms small colonies.

Macrosiphonia macrosiphon (Torr.) Heller
Dogbane (Apocynaceae)

RANGE	6, 7, 10
SIZE	6–12 inches
BLOOMS	May–Sept., Perennial

13 · Blackfoot Daisy

Blackfoot daisy is one of the most drought-tolerant plants in Texas. It blooms from spring through summer, on gravelly or rocky soils, in cracks of rocks, and on slopes and ledges. In flower, it looks like a little white bouquet along the roadside. Each branch of the woody stems ends in a single, one-inch flower head, centered with a yellow disk. The seven to thirteen petals are notched at the tips. Look just under each petal to see a small bract, shaped like a foot.

Jean E. Hardy

These bracts turn black at maturity; thus the common name. The linear leaves of blackfoot daisies are opposite, narrow, and may be slightly lobed. Short, rough hairs coat the leaves and stems.

Melampodium leucanthum T. & G.
Sunflower Family (Asteraceae)

RANGE	5, 7, 8, 9, 10
SIZE	1 foot
BLOOMS	Mar.–Nov., Perennial

14 · White Snakeroot

Harry T. Cliffe

RANGE	1, 2, 3, 4, 7
SIZE	1–5 feet
BLOOMS	July–Oct., Perennial

White snakeroot flower heads form tight clusters. The stalked, alternate leaves are ovate and toothed, with prominent veins. The stems, from a small perennial root-stock, die back each year. White snakeroot is found in many moist habitats, including woodlands, stream and lake banks, ditches, and other poorly drained areas. It some-times forms large colonies and can be found in sun or shade. Named because of its supposed powers of curing snakebite, all parts of this plant are poisonous, fresh or dry. Cattle that graze it become subject to "trembles." The poison, soluble in milk, can be transmitted to persons drinking it, making it the probable cause of the "milk sickness" of early settlers.

Eupatorium rugosum Houtt.
Sunflower Family (Asteraceae)

15 · Anemone, Windflower

Betty Allison Cawlfield

RANGE	1, 2, 3, 4, 5, 6, 7, 8, 10
SIZE	6–20 inches
BLOOMS	Jan.–Apr., Perennial

Blooming earlier than nearly any other flower, anemones bring the promise of spring. Ranging in colors from white, pink, violet, and blue to purple, the wheel-shaped flowers are one and one-half inches across, and appear at the tips of unbranched stems. Ten to thirty petal-like sepals encircle a cylinder, which elongates to one and one-half inches as the flower matures. Between a basal rosette of leaves and the flower, a whorl of much smaller leaves surrounds the stalk. Three species of anemones are found in Texas. They grow mostly in grassy areas, their flowers opening in the sun and closing at night.

Anemone decapetala (Nutt.)
Buttercup Family (Ranunculaceae)

16 · Bush Sunflower

Bush sunflower is a scraggly, bushy plant, widespread in those regions where it occurs. The stiff spreading hairs on its stout stems and leaves feel rough to the touch and effectively protect the species by discouraging grazing animals. Yellow flower heads an inch or more across have both disk and ray flowers. The opposite leaves are triangular in general shape, shallowly lobed, and about an inch long. The half-inch petiole, or leaf stalk, often is broadly winged where it meets the stem. Bush sunflower is found on upland limestone soils.

Simsia calva (Engelm. & Gray) Gray
Sunflower Family (Asteraceae)

Harry T. Cliffe

RANGE	2, 5, 6, 7, 10
SIZE	6–24 inches
BLOOMS	Apr.–Oct., Perennial

Vernon L. Wesby

Scrambled eggs takes its name from its color and the fact that the blossoms at the top of each stem are so irregularly placed that they look stirred. The upper petal has a spur, so the flower seems not to be attached. Alternate leaves are three to six inches long, divided into five to seven segments, then divided twice more. It grows in sandy or rocky areas, prairies, fields, or woods, and along streams or roadsides, especially in disturbed areas. *Corydalis* species found in Texas are difficult to distinguish. They may carry as many as ten alkaloids, and at least one known alkaloid in *Corydalis* is still used in medicine. Plants are poisonous to sheep and are suspected of being poisonous to horses.

Corydalis spp.
Fumitory Family (Fumariaceae)

RANGE	1, 2, 3, 4, 5, 6, 7, 8, 9, 10
SIZE	2 feet
BLOOMS	Feb.–Sept., Annual/Biennial

Harry T. Cliffe

Baptisia species are branching, bushy plants, their flowers often in spikes or racemes. Erect stalks grow from rhizomes. Wild indigo has fifteen to twenty three-quarter-inch yellow, bonnet-like flowers on a stem, each subtended by large floral bracts. Leaves are made up of three leaflets about an inch long. The thick, woody pods stand out prominently on a stalk. After frost, the plant breaks off at the ground and becomes a "tumbleweed." Wild indigo is common on prairies, pastures, and edges of woodlands, growing in loamy, sandy, or silty soils. Continuing hybridization makes finding genetically pure species difficult. Some species may be toxic to livestock.

Baptisia leucophaea Nutt.
Legume Family (Fabaceae)

RANGE	1, 2, 3, 4, 5
SIZE	4 feet
BLOOMS	Apr.–May, Perennial

19 · Puccoon

Susan Sander

This little plant is distinctive because of the ruffled edges on the lobes of its bright yellow, trumpet-shaped flowers. The trumpets are sometimes more than an inch long and up to three-fourths of an inch across, in terminal clusters. They produce no seed. Later in the spring or summer, three or four large, white, stone-like seeds are produced by small, self-pollinating flowers hidden in the bracts. A rosette of linear leaves that give rise to the stem usually withers by bloom time, but smaller leaves farther up the stem may be three inches long and are fuzzy, as is the stem. Puccoon root yields a red dye. A tea brewed from this plant was used as birth control in the past, and several hormone-like molecules have been identified from its juices. Puccoon is one of many native herbs being studied for potential medicinal value.

Lithospermum incisum Lehm.
Borage Family (Boraginaceae)

RANGE	1, 2, 3, 4, 5, 6, 7, 8, 9, 10
SIZE	1 foot
BLOOMS	Nov.–June, Perennial

20 · Texas Greeneyes

Greeneyes is found on sandy or caliche slopes, bluffs, roadsides, or streamsides. Stems and leaves are covered with soft hairs. The triangular, alternate leaves have toothed edges and may have short stems, or none. Daisy-like yellow flowers, two inches across, usually have eight rays or petals, which are notched at a narrow tip, but they can have a few more or less. The center disk is light yellow to greenish, becoming red to maroon as the disk florets open. Flower heads are loosely clus-

tered. A deep taproot gives greeneyes the drought tolerance sought for a xeric garden or landscape. It blooms over a long period of time.

Berlandiera texana DC.
Sunflower Family (Asteraceae)

RANGE	2, 4, 5, 6, 7, 8, 9
SIZE	2–4 feet
BLOOMS	Apr.–Nov., Perennial

Plants of the *Hymenopappus* species have a soft, lacy look. *H. filifolius*, shown, is the only Texas species that is perennial; only one Texas species, *H. biennis*, has petals. Many Texas species are yellow, but they can range from yellow to white, pinkish to wine. They flower in terminal clusters. From a woody taproot, stems may be single or several, branching in the upper part. Some plants are densely covered in white hairs, suggesting the common name "woolly-white." In nature, woolly-white may grow singly,

Vernon L. Wesby

but it is often seen in large stands along roadsides, in abandoned areas, or in pastures. In a wildflower garden, its fern-like foliage provides a soft contrast to coarser plants.

Hymenopappus filifolius Hook.
Sunflower Family (Asteraceae)

RANGE	9
SIZE	6–18 inches
BLOOMS	May–Sept., Perennial

There are at least eight species of *Thelesperma* in Texas. All species have opposite leaves, which are divided once, twice, or sometimes thrice, into segments that are ultimately linear and threadlike. Greenthread has eight yellow, three-lobed, ray flowers around a yellow or brown disk. Occasionally there may be a diffuse brown or reddish brown color near the base of the rays, but never in a definite spot. Indians made a tea from this plant, as well as other *Thelesperma* species,

Zoe M. Kirkpatrick

hence they all are sometimes called "Navajo tea." Some people prefer this tea to commercial varieties. *Thelesperma* is found in dry soils in pastures, prairies, vacant lots, and on roadsides.

Thelesperma filifolium (Hook.) Gray
Sunflower Family (Asteraceae)

RANGE	1,2,4,6,7,8,9, 10
SIZE	8–30 inches
BLOOMS	Feb.–Dec., Perennial

23 · Giant Goldenrod

Harry T. Cliffe

RANGE	1, 2, 3, 4, 5, 6, 7, 8, 9, 10
SIZE	1–6 feet
BLOOMS	July–Nov., Perennial

Across the state, beautiful goldenrods hint that fall is soon to come. Positive identification is difficult; even botanists have trouble with them. They are well known for hybridizing. All have rhizomatous roots that spread, so large colonies are common. Long, slender stems branch in the upper portion. These branches bear branchlets on which tiny yellow flowers are densely clustered. Stalkless leaves alternate up the stems. Goldenrod is wrongly blamed for hay fever; insects, not the wind, carry its pollen. It is said that Indians used a tea from this plant in the treatment of digestive ailments. Goldenrod flowers yield a natural dye, shading from yellow to yellow-green. *S. gigantea* (pictured) is not found in Region 6, but several other goldenrod species can be seen there.

Solidago gigantea Ait. **Sunflower Family (Asteraceae)**

24 · Manystem False Dandelion

RANGE	1, 2, 3, 5, 6, 7, 8
SIZE	6–20 inches
BLOOMS	Feb.–Sept., Annual

The three species of false dandelion generally found in Texas are *P. multicaulis* (pictured) and *P. carolinianus,* both annuals, and *P. grandiflorus,* a perennial. Terminal flowers have layers of many yellow petals around a center sprinkled with dark anther tubes. Flowers open in the morning and usually close around noon. The seed heads form the familiar poof-balls of silvery hairs that children love to blow to the wind. The very small leaves of early spring are sometimes used in salads. They also can be cooked as a potherb, parboiled to

Harry T. Cliffe

take away the bitter taste. While homeowners may think the favored habitat of false dandelion is the family lawn, one species or another can be found on roadsides or prairies, and in pastures and fields, throughout the state. True dandelion, *Tarax-acum,* is not a Texas native, but was introduced in the state and is usually seen in disturbed areas in town or around human habitation.

Pyrrhopappus multicaulis DC. **Sunflower Family (Asteraceae)**

25 · Broomweed

Broomweed grows from a single slender stem, branching to form a loose mass in the upper part. Its tiny, yellow, daisy-like flowers measure about a half-inch across, and are scattered over the plant. From seven to fifteen ray flowers surround the yellow disk flowers. Very narrow, linear leaves alternate up the stem, becoming fewer and shorter toward the top. Often an indicator of overgrazed pastures, broomweed can cover hundreds of acres. It is toxic to livestock, remaining where more palatable plants are no longer seen.

Amphiachyris dracunculoides (DC.) Nutt.
Sunflower Family (Asteraceae)

Zoe M. Kirkpatrick

RANGE	1, 2, 3, 4, 5, 6, 7, 8, 9, 10
SIZE	6–36 inches
BLOOMS	June–Nov., Annual

26 · Curlycup Gumweed

Harry T. Cliffe

Curlycup gumweed is a bushy plant with small, bright, blue-green leaves. It can be found in many habitats, ranging from dry and rocky to moist, sandy areas; it grows along roadsides, fence rows, in pastures, and on prairies. Yellow flowers are about three-fourths to one inch across and may have ray flowers, but the disk flowers bloom from a cup notable for the little downward-bent bracts that cover it. A sticky resin is exuded by the plant, rendering it unpalatable to cattle. Early settlers and Indians used curlycup gumweed medicinally to relieve symptoms of asthma and bronchitis, and to treat poison ivy. *Grindelia* species also yield a natural dye.

Grindelia squarrosa (Pursh.) Dun .
Sunflower Family (Asteraceae)

RANGE	1, 3, 4, 5, 7, 8, 9, 10
SIZE	3 feet
BLOOMS	July–Oct., Perennial

27 · Gordon Bladderpod

Vernon L. Wesby

The characteristic feature of the bladder pods is the small, pea-sized pod that will "pop" when stepped on, illustrating another common name, popweed. The eighteen Texas species vary in size. Most bladderpods are annuals, as is *L. gordonii*, but a few species are biennial, and some are perennial. Identification depends on features of the seedpods and the stalks that support them. The flowers are too uniform and the leaves too variable to be useful in identification. Bladderpods are in the mustard family. They have four petals, opposite each other in pairs, forming a cross, giving the family its former Latin name, *Cruciferae*. Flowers are generally yellow, although some are white. Seeds of bladderpod may be used as a peppery seasoning, or tender leaves can be added to salads of potherbs for a spicy-hot addition. Seeds also yield oil that can be used as a substitute for castor oil.

Lesquerella gordonii (Gray) S. Wats.
Mustard Family (Brassicaceae)

RANGE	5, 6, 7, 8, 9, 10
SIZE	2–12 inches
BLOOMS	Mar.–June, Annual

28 · Showy Buttercup

There are about four hundred buttercup species worldwide, and many have invaded America. The Latin name, *Ranunculus*, means "little frog," and the plants enjoy the same habitat as amphibians. All species are acrid. Some are poisonous to grazing animals, and the juice of some can blister the skin. Flowers are solitary at the end of a stalk, with five or more petals, and they are yellow or white, rarely reddish or green. Yellow-flowered species have a waxy patina because of a peculiar layer of cells beneath the surface. At least one species can be found in each region of Texas.

Dorothy Baird Mattiza

R. macranthus (pictured) has eight to eighteen cupped petals, layered so that they appear semi-double. The flower may be more than an inch across. Stems can be erect reclining, or often creeping.

Ranunculus macranthus Scheele.
Buttercup Family (Ranunculaceae)

RANGE	2, 3, 4, 5, 6, 7, 10
SIZE	12–36 inches
BLOOMS	Feb.–June, Perennial

Texas star is the only species of *Lindheimera* that grows in Texas. It is a bristly, hairy plant, and precocious, known to flower when it is only two inches high. The flower heads, about an inch across, each have four or five bright-yellow ray flowers in a star shape. From the base of each petal, two linear veins extend to the deeply notched tip. One or more flowers tip the leafy stems. The lower leaves alternate and are coarsely toothed, but the upper ones are opposite and smooth on the edges. Also called Lindheimer daisy or yellow star, this plant is found on plains and prairies, in woods, and on roadsides in northeastern and central Texas. It is easily cultivated and makes an attractive garden plant.

Lindheimera texana Gray
Sunflower Family (Asteraceae)

Edith Bettinger

RANGE	2, 3, 4, 5, 7, 8
SIZE	4–24 inches
BLOOMS	Mar.–May, Annual

30 · Halfshrub Sundrops

Halfshrub sundrops, or day primrose (*Calylophus*), is identified by a rounded stigma, as opposed to evening primrose (*Oenothera* spp.), which has a cross-shaped stigma. The bright yellow flowers, sometimes with black centers, are up to two inches across and remain open during the day. The stigma may be black or yellow and extends above the stamens. Plants have woody stems near the base, and the alternate leaves have smooth or toothed margins. The flowers are borne in the axils of the upper leaves. Because of the four-angled buds, this plant is sometimes called square-bud primrose.

Vernon L. Wesby

Calylophus berlandieri Spach.
Evening Primrose Family (Onaraceae)

RANGE	1, 2, 3, 4, 5, 6, 7, 8, 9, 10
SIZE	6–32 inches
BLOOMS	Mar.–June, Perennial

31 · Desert Baileya

Desert baileya forms a clump of basal leaves covered with woolly-white hairs. The stems, bare of leaves, rise above the gray-green foliage in a spray, each holding a chrome-yellow flower head that seems to face the sky. Flowers, an inch and one-half across, have twenty-five to fifty ray flowers multi-layered around a large, flat disk. Because its faded flowers dry to a parchment color and remain on the plant, desert baileya is sometimes called paper-daisy, but it shouldn't be confused with several other species that sometimes carry the same common name. The plant is poisonous to sheep, although it does not seem to affect other animals. Ribbons of these yellow flowers flank miles of desert highways for much of the year. There are few floral displays more spectacular than the mingling of bluebonnets and desert baileya in the spring.

Vernon L. Wesby

Baileya multiradiata Harv. & Gray
Sunflower Family (Asteraceae)

RANGE	7, 10
SIZE	8–18 inches
BLOOMS	Jan.–Dec., Annual/Perennial

32 · Maximilian Sunflower

Sunflowers are among the most easily recognized plants, yet species may be difficult to distinguish because of hybridizing. All have large flower heads with yellow, or occasionally reddish, ray flowers surrounding a flattened, yellow or rust-colored disk. Maximilian sunflower is a particularly attractive species, with many three-inch flowers opening at the same time, in leaf axils of the upper third of the plants. It has tall, stout, hairy stems and leaves. Colonies of Maximilian sunflowers make a dramatic fall display, in roadside swales, seasonally moist meadows and prairies, and along fencerows. Sunflowers are useful; the oil is commercially important and the thickened roots of Maximilian sunflower are edible raw, boiled, or roasted. A nutritious plant, it was believed by Indians to have medicinal value, and it is now recognized as valuable in wildlife habitat restoration.

Edith Bettinger

Helianthus maximiliani Schrad.
Sunflower Family (Asteraceae)

RANGE	1, 2, 3, 4, 5, 7, 8, 9, 10
SIZE	3–10 feet
BLOOMS	July–Oct., Perennial

It's too bad this little plant limits itself to just three regions in Texas, because it is most attractive and showy. Plains zinnia forms a low, rounded clump or mound of bright yellow that lasts most of the summer, gradually fading to an ivory hue. The blossoms are an inch or more across, with three to six petals around a high disk of eighteen to twenty-four red or green disk flowers. Alternate leaves are tiny, green, and very narrow, forming a moss-like mat when not in bloom. In the landscape, plains zinnia is ideal for a border or rock garden, and it is excellent for erosion control and medians. It can be confused with paperflowers in the genus *Psilostrophe*, but paperflowers are distinguished

Zoe M. Kirkpatrick

by the three-toothed tips of their petals. *Z. acerosa*, or dwarf zinnia, is native from the Trans-Pecos to the Rio Grande Valley, and it is similar except for its white flowers and silvery foliage.

Zinnia grandiflora Nutt.
Sunflower Family (Asteraceae)

RANGE	8, 9, 10
SIZE	8 inches
BLOOMS	May.–Oct., Perennial

Bitterweed is so named because of the flavor it imparts to milk of cows that graze it. The plant is toxic, especially to sheep. Because of its noxious taste, it is not often browsed except during times of drought or in overstocked pastures. Leaves and stems exude a resin-like liquid, which gives the plant a peculiar odor. Bitterweed is many-branched, and its compact mounds are covered with yellow flowers. Flower heads are solitary on stalks. Each has six to thirteen ray flowers that widen

Zoe M. Kirkpatrick

at the toothed tips. They surround a center "button" supporting yellow-orange disk flowers less than one-fourth of an inch tall. It is common in fields, along roadsides, and in roadside ditches.

Hymenoxys odorata DC.
Sunflower Family (Asteraceae)

RANGE	3, 4, 5, 6, 7, 8, 9, 10
SIZE	4–24 inches
BLOOMS	Feb.–June, Perennial

35 · Sawtooth Daisy

RANGE	1, 3, 4, 5, 7, 8, 9, 10
SIZE	2–5 feet
BLOOMS	Aug.–Nov., Annual

Betty Allison Cawlfield

Sawtooth daisy is a stout, erect plant. Its stems branch near the top, with each branch supporting several crowded flowers near its end. Stalkless alternate leaves are thick, with coarse, sharply toothed edges. The stems are ridged and stiff. The plant is sticky; it derives another common name, gumweed, from the sap that oozes from any wound. Indians used to collect, ball, and chew this sap. Flower heads of sawtooth daisy are about an inch or more across, with many yellow petals and disk flowers. Plants are found on roadsides, plains, prairies, in deserted areas, and in fields.

Prionopsis ciliata (Nutt.) Nutt.
Sunflower Family (Asteraceae)

36 · Engelmann Daisy

When you drive through Texas in May, this plant seems to be everywhere, but take another look! It flowers from the roadside to the fence line, but not on the other side where there are livestock. Engelmann daisy is so rich in protein (nearly 27 percent) that animals love it, and it is being utilized in the restoration of rangeland. A deep taproot enables this plant to survive drought conditions and to bloom nearly year-round, with one- to two-inch lemon-yellow flowers. The eight to ten ray flowers are indented at the tip. Both the stout stems and alternating leaves are covered with hairs. Basal leaves are six to twelve inches long, decreasing in size up the stem. The leaf blade is long-stalked and deeply cut or lobed, hence another common name, "cutleaf daisy."

Engelmannia pinnatifida Nutt. ex Nutt.
Sunflower Family (Asteraceae)

RANGE	2, 3, 4, 5, 6, 7, 8, 9, 10
SIZE	1 1/2 – 3 1/2 feet
BLOOMS	Feb.–Nov., Perennial

37 · Stiffstem Flax

While the flax family is widespread, only one genus is represented in Texas. Seventeen species and several varieties give the genus broad distribution, and each corner of the state hosts at least one species. Valued through history, flax (the English translation of the Latin word *Linum*) contains the fibers from which linen is produced. Linseed oil comes from the seed. *L. rigidum*, stiffstem flax, shown, is found throughout Texas and is frequently seen in grassy areas and along roadsides. Its cupped flowers are yellow to copper-colored, often with a dark reddish center and red veins extending up the petals. Leaves are alternate, stalkless, needle-like, and approximately an inch long. All species of wild flax are delicate in appearance, with small, linear leaves. Their flowers range in size from one-fourth to one and one-half inches across, and have five petals. Most are blue; others are yellow or pink.

Zoe M. Kirkpatrick

Linum rigidum Pursh
Flax Family (Linaceae)

RANGE	Range: 1, 2, 3, 4, 5, 6, 7, 8, 9, 10
SIZE	8–20 inches
BLOOMS	Feb.–Sept., Annual

38 · Mexican Hat

Mexican hat is perhaps the most easily identified of all the wildflowers. Its "sombrero," an elongated disk sometimes two inches high, sets Mexican hat apart from other coneflowers. The disk/column is gray-green at first, turning brown as it matures. Drooping, velvety petals surround its base. Petal color varies from all yellow to all red-brown or assorted mixtures of red-brown painted on a yellow petal. The lacy foliage is deeply divided into almost thread-like segments. Leaves up to six inches alternate up slender stems, but the top third of the stem is bare, accenting the flower head.

Zoe M. Kirkpatrick

Ratibida columnifera (Nutt.) Woot. & Standl.
Sunflower Family (Asteraceae)

RANGE	1, 2, 3, 4, 5, 6, 7, 8, 9, 10
SIZE	1–4 feet
BLOOMS	Feb.–July, Perennial

39 · Plains Coreopsis

Laurence Parent

Plains coreopsis is seen as large splashes of yellow along roadsides and in fields in spring, especially in relatively moist soils. It is sometimes spectacularly mixed with Texas paintbrush and bluebonnets. The plants produce numerous flower heads on slender, branching stems. Brown centers are flecked with yellow. Ray petals are yellow with a maroon spot at the base, which may be small or may occupy a large part of the ray. There are many species with several varieties of coreopsis in Texas, often making identification difficult. Although its big show is in the spring, coreopsis will bloom until frost in a year with ample rains.

Coreopsis tinctoria Nutt.
Sunflower Family (Asteraceae)

RANGE	1, 2, 3, 4, 5, 6, 7, 8, 9, 10
SIZE	1–4 feet
BLOOMS	Feb.–Dec., Annual

40 · Cowpen Daisy

Yellow, daisy-like flower heads with prominent, yellow-orange centers top the slender stems of this bushy composite. A covering of hair gives the stems and foliage a blue-green or gray-green appearance. Flowers vary in size to two and one-half inches across, and there are three deeply cut teeth at the tips of each of the twelve to sixteen petals. Thick leaves are shaped like arrowheads, coarsely toothed on the edges, and prominently veined on the underside. A Spanish name, *anil del muerto*, meaning "sunflower of the dead," was given to this plant because of its strong, unpleasant odor when crushed. A salve made from cowpen daisy has been used as an anti-inflammatory agent; cowpen tea is said to relieve an early peptic ulcer, and some

believe it may break a fever by inducing sweating and relaxation. Its seeds have high oil content.

Verbesina encelioides (Cav.) Benth. & Hook.
Sunflower Family (Asteraceae)

RANGE	2, 3, 4, 5, 6, 7, 8, 9, 10
SIZE	1–4 feet
BLOOMS	Feb.–Dec., Annual

41 · Black-Eyed Susan

Black-eyed Susan is named for the brown center disk, which may rise an inch above the petals. Slightly drooping petals are yellow, often with a dash of reddish brown near their base. Tips of the eight to twenty petals may be toothed. Stems and leaves are covered with rough hairs. Leaves are unlobed, narrowed at the base, variable in shape, but usually longer than broad, and sometimes obscurely toothed. The stems usually branch at the mid-point. Black-eyed Susan grows in various types of soil but especially favors sandy or alluvial soils. It is found in grassy areas along roadsides, and at the edges of woods. It is utilized for dye and tea and Indians are believed to have used juice from its roots to relieve earaches.

Rudbeckia hirta L.
Sunflower Family (Asteraceae)

RANGE	1, 2, 4, 7
SIZE	1–3 feet
BLOOMS	May–Nov., Annual/Perennial

Robert & Linda Mitchell

42 · Indian Blanket

As Texas's annual spring bluebonnet show fades, Indian blankets begin to bloom. Acre upon acre of them can be seen in fields, pastures, and on roadsides. The ancestor of several cultivated varieties, *Gaillardia* is now planted along interstate highways; seasonal color of wildflowers along the right-of-way has proven to be practical as well as beautiful, saving the cost of constant mowing. This flashy flower tops a bushy little plant, with two-inch wheels of red petals tipped with yellow. The center disk starts out yellow, turning dark red with age. Flowers are solitary on a stem. Of the seven *Gaillardia* species in Texas, this one and *G. amblyodon* are annual; the others are all perennial. Flower colors can vary from all red to all yellow.

Gaillardia pulchella Foug.
Sunflower Family (Asteraceae)

Jean E. Hardy

RANGE	1, 2, 3, 4, 5, 6, 7, 8, 9, 10
SIZE	1–2½ feet
BLOOMS	Feb.–Dec., Annual

43 · Texas Lantana

Lantanas are often seen along fencerows or under telephone or power lines where birds perch. The shiny, blue-black, fleshy, eighth- to quarter-inch fruits are potentially lethal to people and livestock. They are, however, readily eaten by birds, which subsequently drop the seeds in fertilized pellets to sprout and beautify the countryside. Additionally, lantana is an important source of nectar. The three- to five-foot woody plants have small, funnel-shaped, orange flowers surrounding yellow flowers, all in densely clustered small globes that turn red as they age. The stems, square when young, become rounded with maturity, and may become slightly prickly. Oval to triangular leaves are one to three inches long and have coarsely toothed margins. *L. camara* is a pink- and yellow-flowered plant from the West Indies that has escaped cultivation and is now found throughout much of Texas.

Lantana horrida Kunth in H.B.K.
Verbena Family (Verbenaceae)

RANGE	1, 2, 3, 4, 5, 6, 7, 10
SIZE	3–5 feet
BLOOMS	Mar.–Oct., Perennial

44 · Standing Cypress

Feathery, light green foliage topped with a thick, red-orange spike of trumpet-shaped flowers ensures that standing cypress will always be noticed in bloom, as will its Trans-Pecos cousin, skyrocket gilia (*I. aggregata*). Both species grow in sun or partial shade. Flowers open from the top of the spike downward. They have five lobes, pointed or rounded, that flare flat, (from tubes to one and one-half inches long). The inside of the flower is mottled or spotted. A basal rosette of the first year's fern-like foliage gives rise the second year to a flowering stalk, which has alternate leaves dissected into threadlike segments. The plant reseeds readily before dying. Standing cypress is often seen in large colonies, and it is an important food source for hummingbirds.

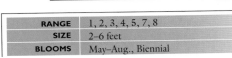

Ipomopsis rubra (l.) Wherry
Phlox Family (Polemoniaceae)

RANGE	1, 2, 3, 4, 5, 7, 8
SIZE	2–6 feet
BLOOMS	May–Aug., Biennial

This brilliantly colored, clump-forming milkweed attracts butterflies, hummingbirds, and other pollinators to its sweet nectar. Its hairy stems are often branched in the upper portions and capped with numerous clusters of tiny orange, red-orange, or yellow flowers. The seeds and roots of butterfly milkweed are said to have mild laxative properties, and a tea made from the root is thought to be useful for heart problems. Indians chewed the root like gum, yet the leaves are poisonous to livestock. While butterfly milkweed has a wide range in varied habitats from prairies and fields to thickets, it is rarely found in the West.

Asclepias tuberosa L.
Milkweed Family (Asclepiadaceae)

Jeffery G. Schultz

RANGE	1, 2, 3, 4, 5, 6, 7, 8, 9, 10
SIZE	3 feet
BLOOMS	Apr.–Sept., Perennial

46 · Globe Mallow, False Mallow

Even the professional botanist has difficulty in identifying individual species of globe mallows (*Sphaeralcea*), and the task is practically impossible for the amateur. There are slight differences between many species, and in nature they readily hybridize. As a group, globe mallows can be recognized quite easily. They are upright and hairy, with star-shaped (stellate) hairs on the stems and leaves. The alternate leaf-blades of *S. angustifolia* are linear, toothed, and long-stalked, and may be more than three inches long. Flowers are clustered, each on a short stem, along a central stalk. The flowers are five-petaled, cupped slightly, and may be dark yellow, salmon, bright orange to pink, or lavender. Different colors will often be found, even in one group of plants presumably of the same species. Mallows have been used medicinally as poultices, and the stems are chewed like gum. They do well in cultivation.

Sphaeralcea angustifolia (Cav.) G. Don
Mallow Family (Malvaceae)

Jean E. Hardy

RANGE	7, 8, 9, 10
SIZE	1–6 feet
BLOOMS	Jan.–Dec., Perennial

47 · Cupleaf Penstemon

Betty Allison Cawlfield

RANGE	1, 2, 3, 4, 7
SIZE	2–6 feet
BLOOMS	Mar.–June, Perennial

Cupleaf penstemon is stately and extremely showy. Bright red-orange blossoms grow in pairs on short stems, from a cupped pair of bracts fused at the stalk. The flowering spike may be a foot or more long, with each inch-long, tubular flower having an upper, two-lobed lip and a lower, three-lobed lip. Lower, opposite leaves are spatula-shaped or oblong, fleshy, and bluish green, becoming more or less round on the upper part of the stems. Cupleaf penstemon usually grows in sandy soils, on the edges of pine or oak woods, and in open prairies. About three hundred species of penstemon are indigenous to America, from Alaska to Guatemala. Twenty-two of these are found in Texas.

Penstemon murrayanus Hook
Figwort Family (Scrophulariaceae)

48 · Texas Paintbrush

Nine species of paintbrush are found in Texas, but this is the only annual one. The conspicuous parts of the plant are the bracts, subtending and concealing the slender, one-inch, yellow-green flowers. Together they form showy three- to eight-inch terminal spikes. The bracts are brilliant red to red-orange, or orange. Alternate leaves are one to four inches long, and both stems and leaves are hairy. Texas paintbrush is frequently planted along interstate highways. Mixed with

bluebonnets and an occasional white prickly poppy, it makes one of the state's most outstanding spring wildflower displays.

Castilleja indivisa Engelm.
Figwort Family (Scrophulariaceae)

RANGE	1, 2, 3, 4, 5, 6, 7
SIZE	6–18 inches
BLOOMS	Mar.–May, Annual

Cardinal flower is usually less than four feet tall and is found in wetlands, near streams, roadside ditches, and ponds. The fall-blooming flower is an important food source for migrating hummingbirds, its chief pollinators, and for many butterflies. Scarlet, tubular flowers bloom along the top third of the leafy, unbranched stem. They open into five lobes, the upper two of which are longer and narrower than the lower three. Flowering spires may reach eighteen inches in length, and individual flowers are more than an inch long. Alternate leaves are simple, egg-shaped to lanceolate, with toothed margins. Species of *Lobelia* contain alkaloids that are potentially lethal to people, and the plants are poisonous to goats and cattle.

Lobelia cardinalis L.
Bluebell Family (Campanulaceae)

Jean E. Hardy

RANGE	1, 2, 3, 4, 5, 6, 7, 8, 9, 10
SIZE	3–5 feet
BLOOMS	July–Oct., Perennial

50 · Tropical Sage

Tropical sage is an upright, aromatic, hairy plant with square stems typical of the mint family. Bright red flowers are about an inch long and two-lipped, with the upper lip narrow and extended forward. The lower lip is broad and three-lobed. Flowers are in clusters of well-separated whorls that form a long, slender spike. Leaves are opposite and stalked, saw- toothed, or scalloped on the margins. Other red *Salvias* in the state are *S. roemeriana*, usually found in shaded, rocky woods, with erect to reclining stems; *S. greggii*, a woody shrub of west Texas; *S. regla*, found in the Chisos Mountains, and *S. penstemonoides*, a rare Edwards Plateau endemic. Their flowers attract many pollinators, especially hummingbirds. A long flowering season makes them a reliable source of nectar. As the name "sage" implies, *Salvia* can be used as a condiment, or the leaves dried for tea. *Salvia* is represented in Texas by twenty-one species, six of which are shrubs.

Salvia coccinia Buchoz ex Etlinger
Mint Family (Lamiaceae)

Mark Barnett

RANGE	1, 2, 3, 4, 6, 7, 8
SIZE	1-3 feet
BLOOMS	Mar.–Dec., Perennial

51 · Scarlet Muskflower

Jean E. Hardy

Scarlet muskflower has horizontally spreading, sticky, jointed stems a foot or more long, which bear thick, wavy, ovate, or triangular leaves on long stalks. Plants are conspicuously hairy. If you bend down to smell the flowers, you'll discover the offensive scent that gives it another common name, "devil's bouquet." Flowers are in clusters one and one-half to three inches across, opening in the evening and closing in the morning. The fruits are about one-fourth of an inch across and are eaten by many kinds of birds. Scarlet muskflower is widely scattered on the calcareous or limestone soils across southwest Texas.

Nyctaginia capitata Choisy
Four-O'Clock Family (Nyctaginaceae)

RANGE	2, 5, 6, 7, 8, 10
SIZE	6 inches
BLOOMS	Mar.–Nov., Perennial

52 · Turk's Cap

Turk's cap may be erect or sprawling and is usually widely branched. The shallow-lobed leaves are two to four inches long, about as broad, and are rather velvety underneath. Each bright red flower has five petals, one to two inches long, that remain spirally closed as in a rosebud. From the center of the flower, the stamens form a conspicuous, pollen-producing column that extends an inch or two beyond the petals. While it is still flowering, the plant bears red, berry-like fruits, edible but bland. Turk's cap often forms large colonies on the margins of woods near rivers and streams. It attracts butterflies in great numbers. In native landscaping, it is a useful, dramatic plant for shady or partially shady locations. The Texas variety (*M. arboreus Drummondii*) is so distinctive that many authors consider it a separate species.

Malvaviscus arboreus Cav.
Mallow Family (Malvaceae)

Dorothy Baird Mattiza

RANGE	2, 3, 4, 5, 6, 7
SIZE	2–4 feet
BLOOMS	June–Oct., Perennial

RANGE	1
SIZE	3 feet
BLOOMS	July–Oct., Perennial

An unusual, delightful plant, catchfly gives the effect of red fireflies in the daytime on the edge of a dark, moist wood. While it is not considered rare, *S. subciliata* is not common; it is included because it is one you will be certain to wonder about should you happen upon it. Leaves are long and narrow, rather fleshy, but sparse. The plant is inconspicuous except for the glowing scarlet flowers at the end of slender stems. Flowers are tubular, flaring into five equal, narrow lobes. They are about one and one-half inches across and have

Jeffery G. Schultz

protruding stamens. *S. subciliata* grows only in east Texas. At the western extreme of the state, another catchfly (*S. laciniata*) is found in gravelly, shady places in the Chisos and Davis mountains. Also called "fire pink," this western species has five fringed, scarlet, petal-like lobes, each deeply notched into four narrow sections.

Silene subciliata Robins
Pink Family (Caryophyllaceae)

54 · Trailing Ratany

Jeffery G. Schultz

RANGE	2, 3, 4, 5, 6, 7, 8, 9, 10
SIZE	2 feet
BLOOMS	Apr.–Oct., Perennial

Although you may never notice this little plant unless you look underfoot at the right time, trailing ratany is easy to identify when in bloom. It has iridescent, dime-sized, orchid-like flowers with five large, wine-colored sepals, surrounding five inconspicuous, true petals. Its inch-long, silky leaves are alternate and very narrow. The fruit, a downy, round bur with delicate spines, contains only one seed. Ratany does not get very large. It has a woody base, with stems trailing like a semivine. The dried root, tinctured, is an effective astringent.

Krameria lanceolata Torr.
Ratany Family (Krameriaceae)

55 · Winecup, Low Poppy Mallow

Zoe M. Kirkpatrick

Several species of winecups in Texas vary in color from deep wine to pink or white, but the blossoms are always recognizably similar. They flower on long stalks from leaf axils, at first cup- or goblet-shaped, then flattening out as the blossom matures. Their flowers open at midday and close near dusk, but the exact flowering period may be related to water availability. The incised leaves are shallowly or deeply cut into five to seven lobes and are wider than they are long. Both leaves and flowers of winecup yield a dye, but whether the color is orange or gray depends upon the mordant used. Winecup often grows in mixed stands with other wildflowers.

Callirhoe involucrata (Torr.) Gray
Mallow Family (Malvaceae)

RANGE	1, 2, 3, 4, 5, 6, 7, 8, 9
SIZE	18 inches
BLOOMS	Feb.–July, Perennial

56 · Purslane

Purslane is the little succulent often considered a weed in the garden, although it can be quite showy on barren, sandy sites where it typically grows. Six species of purslane are known in Texas, some with attractive yellow, orange, or pink to purplish flowers. Moss-rose (*P. gandiflora*), with two-inch flowers, is a South American native that has escaped cultivation in Texas. Pussley (*P. oleracea*), thought to be a native of India, has spread nearly worldwide, and has been used as food for more than two thousand years. Shaggy portulaca (another name for the species shown), as well as chisme (*P. pilosa*), were collected by Indians and dried to store for winter use.

Vernon I. Weehy

Portulaca umbraticola H.B.K.
Portulaca Family (Portulacaceae)

RANGE	1, 2, 3, 4, 5, 6, 7, 8, 10
SIZE	2–6 inches
BLOOMS	Mar.–Dec., Annual

57 · Eryngo

This is not a thistle, but wear a pair of gloves if you want to handle it. In August, the eryngo plant turns from gray-green to purple. If cut when the color first changes, then hung upside down in the shade to dry, the color will last for months. The flower head is most unusual, with a two-inch-tall purple cylinder sandwiched between a collar of deeply lobed, spiny bracts and a crown of small, erect, spiny leaves. Stems are leafy and branch widely in the upper portion. The deeply incised leaf blades are stalkless and clasp the stem. The pointed tips have stiff spines. Eryngo grows on clay, limestone, or gravelly soils of plains, prairies, and grassland.

Eryngium leavenworthii T. & G.
Carrot Family (Apiaceae)

Dorothy Baird Mattiza

RANGE	1, 2, 3, 4, 5, 7, 8, 9
SIZE	4 feet
BLOOMS	July–Oct., Annual

58 · Texas Stork's Bill

Stork's bill has horizontal stems. Stalked, wrinkled leaves, indented at the base, are three-lobed and are one to two inches long. The reddish purple flowers, an inch across, have five petals and are in clusters of two or three. Sensitive to light, the flowers open in late afternoon and close in the morning. Fruits are one to three inches long and divide into a v-shaped beak as they mature, reminiscent of the long bill of a stork. Stork's bill can be used as a potherb, or chopped for salads if collected in early spring when it is tender. A tea made of the leaves has been used as a mild diuretic, and is said to relieve gout and rheumatism. It can be found growing in open sandy or rocky places, on prairies, or on disturbed sites.

Erodium texanum Gray
Geranium Family (Geraniaceae)

Jean E. Hardy

RANGE	2, 3, 4, 5, 6, 7, 8, 10
SIZE	6–18 inches
BLOOMS	Feb.–May, Annual/Biennial

59 · Cobaea Penstemon

Kay Warmerdam

Cobaea penstemon is an impressive, clump-forming plant with solitary or several downy stems. It is often found in colonies along roadsides. Plump, tubular flowers may be nearly white, pink, or pale lavender, with purple lines on the floor of the throat. They are clustered in small leaf axils on the upper two-thirds of the stem. Opposite leaves are two to three inches long and waxy-shiny, with coarse teeth on the margins. From midstem upward, leaves become smaller and stalkless. Another common name, beard-tongue, refers to the plant's infertile stamen, which is covered with a "beard" of soft, yellow hairs. Seventeen *Penstemon* species are found across Texas, and are among our showiest flowers. Indians made a penstemon tea to use as a laxative. A salve made of penstemon is used for skin irritations, both in preventive care and as a treatment.

Penstemon cobaea Nutt.
Figwort Family (Scrophulariaceae)

RANGE	2, 3, 4, 5, 6, 7, 8
SIZE	1–2½ feet
BLOOMS	Apr.–June, Perennial

60 · Rough Nama, Sand-Bells

Variable in form, rough nama is freely branching or sprawling from its base. It is covered with short, appressed hairs, making it rough to the touch. Bell-shaped flowers are in small clusters or solitary from the axils of leaves, a half-inch across. They are pink to purple, with a yellow or white throat. The leaves are especially variable, one-half to two inches long, stalked generally linear, but sometimes divided lobed, or toothed, with edges rolled under. They are alternate and have a pungent odor. Masses of the purple flowers are often seen as mats along the shoulders of highways, or wherever gravelly, sandy, or alluvial soils are found. Rough nama is an attractive landscape choice when used in a sunny rock garden or border. Twelve species of *Nama* are found in Texas.

Dorothy Baird Mattiza

Nama hispidum Gray
Waterleaf Family (Hydrophyllaceae)

RANGE	2, 3, 4, 5, 6, 7, 8, 9, 10
SIZE	4–20 inches
BLOOMS	Mar.–Nov., Annual

Prairie rose-gentian usually forms large colonies and is often spectacular in early spring, covering acres of rangeland or painting miles of roadsides with bright color. It is found in full sun, on dry or moist sandy soils, pastures, prairies, flats, and woodland edges. The solitary stems are smooth, branching only in the upper portion. Slender opposite leaves, up to one and one-half inch long, clasp the square stems. Single, short-stemmed flowers grow from the axils of the upper leaves. Bright-pink petals are joined at the base, centered with a yellow star. The five-petaled flowers may reach an inch across. Plants are self-seeding, easily cultivated, and a good garden choice.
Sabatia campestris Nutt.
Gentian Family (Gentianaceae)

Jeffery G. Schultz

RANGE	1, 2, 3, 4, 5, 6, 7, 8, 9
SIZE	5–20 inches
BLOOMS	Mar.–July, Annual

62 · Phlox

One or more species of *Phlox* can be found nearly anywhere in Texas, with twelve species and nineteen subspecies in the state. *Phlox pilosa* is pictured. Individual species may be difficult for the amateur to distinguish, but they are easy to recognize as a group. Color is variable, but most are pink, while others may be white, violet, blue, or red. Five petals flare from an evenly narrow tube to a flattened "tray. " Petals of some species have pointed tips, some are notched, but all widen toward the outer edge. Flowers are numerous, and only a few open at a time from terminal clusters. Leaves are opposite in the lower portion of the plants. Phlox forms broad colonies, and most species reseed readily. These plants are frequently seen with bluebonnet, blue-eyed grass, paintbrush, and other spring wildflowers, brightening the landscape with strong splashes of color.
Phlox spp.
Phlox Family (Polemoniaceae)

Dorothy Baird Mattiza

RANGE	1, 2, 3, 4, 5, 6, 7, 8, 9, 10
SIZE	8–20 inches
BLOOMS	Feb.–June, Annual/Perennial

63 · Gaura

Jean E. Hardy

Considered weedy by some, gaura has alternate leaves borne singly on the stems. Flowers are in spikes or on axillary branches. Bilaterally symmetrical, gaura has four petals on the upper side of the flower, while eight long stamens and one pistil droop from the lower side, giving the flower a whiskered look. Pale flowers, which begin opening from the bottom of the spike upward, turn reddish with age. Most gaura open in the evening or near sunrise for their moth pollinators. Fragrant and rich in nectar, they also attract bees, fly species, and hummingbirds. Look for gaura in sunny gravelly or sandy, well-drained locations.

Gaura spp.
Evening Primrose Family (Onagraceae)

RANGE	1, 2, 3, 4, 5, 6, 7, 8, 9, 10
SIZE	3 feet
BLOOMS	Mar.–July, Annual/Perennial

64 · Showy Primrose

Lax and sprawling, this early spring to summer bloomer has a cup-shaped flower of four petals, united at the base to form a short tube. The pink flowers are two to over three inches across, with a yellow center edged in white. The branching plants, spread by underground rhizomes, form large colonies. Alternate leaves are lobed or cleft, two or three inches long, and toothed or wavy. Showy primrose is easily grown from seed. The flowers of this species open in the evening; some other *Oenothera* species, though also known as evening primroses, actually open in the morning. Evening primroses are often called "buttercups" because of their abundant yellow pollen and the cup-like form of their flowers. An introduction from Europe, *O. biennis*, was once a popular vegetable, cultivated for its roots; it can be found throughout the eastern United States, extending into east Texas. *Oenothera* are not related to true primroses *(Primula)*.

Harry T. Cliffe

Oenothera speciosa L.
Evening Primrose Family (Onagraceae)

RANGE	1, 2, 3, 4, 5, 6, 7, 8,10
SIZE	8–18 inches
BLOOMS	Mar.–July, Perennial

Although thistles are not a farmer's favorite, goldfinches and other birds eat the seed, butterflies and bumblebees are drawn to the nectar; and the larvae of the painted-lady butterfly feed on the foliage. In the great scheme of things, Texas thistle is important. A handsome plant, it has long hairs mixed with disk flowers, making a fluffy, rose-lavender globe that sits in a green bract cup. There is one flower head to a stem. The base of each leaf clasps the hairy stem, and the alternate leaves have spiny-toothed lobes. Upper sides of leaves are dark green, but the underside is woolly. Several species are similar. *Cirsium texanum* Buckl.
Sunflower Family (Asteraceae)

Jean E. Hardy

RANGE	2, 3, 4, 5, 6, 7, 8, 9, 10
SIZE	2–5 feet
BLOOMS	Apr.–Aug., Annual/Perennial

Identifying wild asters by species may be baffling to the amateur naturalist and it often challenges the professional. One authority states that Texas has forty-five species. There are at least six wild blue asters, ranging from blue-white, blue, violet, and lavender to purple. The many-petaled flowers range in size from a half-inch to two inches. Center disks are yellow. Flowers on the upper stems are profuse. Most asters are fall blooming and an important source of late-season nectar for butterflies. A tea made from cured roots of the plant was used by Indians to stop diarrhea. Asters can be seen along edges of woods, on prairies, and along fencerows, where they grow in clay, sand, or gravelly soils.
Aster spp.
Sunflower Family (Asteraceae)

Dorothy Baird Mattiza

RANGE	1, 2, 3, 4, 5, 7
SIZE	1–4 feet
BLOOMS	Aug.–Dec., Perennial

67 · Spotted Beebalm

Jeffery G. Schultz

Monardas are strongly scented and square-stemmed and have opposite leaves. Clustered flowers, each with a large bract at its base, are whorled intermittently up the stem, ending with a cluster at the tip. Spotted beebalm has flowers that are creamy yellow or sometimes pinkish, peppered with tiny light brown or red spots. The bracts subtending the flowers are broad and petal-like, and may be white, yellowish, pale green, or lavender. Thymol, an antiseptic, is derived from an oil of this showy plant. *Monarda* species have been important to people for hundreds of years. Their essential oils have been used medicinally, for flavorings, perfumes, and insect repellents. The leaves have been used for tea and as a garnish. Honey from a beehive near a field of flowering *Monarda* will take on its flavor, a taste too strong for some people, but relished by others. *Monarda* is irresistible to butterflies and other pollinators.

Monarda punctata L.
Mint Family (Lamiaceae)

RANGE	1,2,3,4,5,6,7,8,9,10
SIZE	3 feet
BLOOMS	Apr.–Sept., Annual/Perennial

68 · Rose Mallow, Rose Pavonia

Although uncommon in the wild, pavonia is increasingly appreciated as a desirable garden plant. In the southern part of its range, pavonia may flower all year and remain evergreen. Rosy pink flowers are one and one-half inches across, and are solitary, opening in the morning and closing in early afternoon. Alternate stalked leaves, with margins coarsely toothed or lobed, are one inch to more than two and a half inches long. Velvety leaf blades may be triangle-, heart-, or egg-shaped. The plant is hairy, branching from a solitary stem. Pavonia is found on dry, rocky limestone soils, in a brushy or woodland habitat. Short-lived, it reseeds readily.

Pavonia lasiopetala Scheele.
Mallow Family (Malvaceae)

Andy Wasowski

RANGE	6, 7
SIZE	1–3 feet
BLOOMS	Mar.–Nov., Perennial

All *Palafoxias* are pink to rose, or almost purple, with a single, branched stem bearing single or loosely clustered flower heads. Most are hairy plants, sometimes sticky to touch. Rose palafoxia has no ray flowers; the whole flower head is composed of fluffy disk flowers. It makes its beautiful, airy display in sandy soils, in open areas, and on the edges of woods. Seeds sown in the fall can be used in wildflower meadows or in the landscape. Palafoxia is most effective planted in a mass. The fragrant flowers attract butterflies and other pollinators to a plentiful supply of nectar and pollen. *P. callosa* is an almost identical relative, found across southwestern central to northeastern central parts of the state on limestone soil.

Palafoxia rosea (Bush) Cory
Sunflower Family (Asteraceae)

Betty Allison Cawlfield

RANGE	2, 3, 4, 5, 6, 7, 8, 9
SIZE	2 feet
BLOOMS	June–Nov., Annual

This sprawling plant, with stems to six feet long, is usually covered with prickles. Its sensitive leaves fold immediately upon being touched. They also close on cloudy days and at night. The alternate leaves have blades divided once into four to eight pairs of leaflets, which divide again into eight to fifteen pairs of smaller leaflets. Fuzzy, pink globes, an inch or smaller, are actually congested clusters of fragrant flowers at the tip of a leafless stalk. Sensitive briar can be found on sandy or gravelly roadsides, pastures, prairies, openings, and edges of woods. Its fruit is a prickly bean pod. Six Texas species may interbreed and are considered to be a single species by some botanists.

Vernon L. Wesby

Schrankia nuttallii (Britt. & Rose) Standl.
Legume Family (Fabaceae)

RANGE	1, 2, 3, 4, 5, 6, 7, 8, 9
SIZE	6 feet
BLOOMS	Apr.–Sept., Perennial

71 · Mountain Pink

Kay Warmerdam

There is no need to look very far for mountain pink. This little plant is easy to find because one of its favorite habitats is along the edges of paved roads, where it forms perfect bouquets of pink stars. Individual flowers reach an inch across, and are deeply five-lobed. The plant's flowers and buds are numerous, at the ends or in forks of branches. Lower paired leaves may reach one and one-half inch long and are linear, but the leaves become threadlike in upper branchlets. Mountain pink often appears on rocky slopes and hillsides or open, disturbed areas, probably needing the heat of full sun for seed germination.

Centaurium beyrichii (T.&.G.) Robins.
Gentian Family (Gentianaceae)

RANGE	7, 8, 9, 10
SIZE	4–12 inches
BLOOMS	May–Aug., Annual

72 · Purple Coneflower

Purple coneflower may appear "purple" to some, but the drooping ray flowers vary from very pale pink to dull crimson, yellow in one species, and purplish red in another. The prickly disk is almost flat at first, becoming domed and finally somewhat cone-shaped as it matures. Each flower head is borne on a stiffly erect stem that rises from a basal rosette of sand-papery leaves. Blacksamson, another common name, refers to the thick black root, which was used by Indians to cure wounds and aches. A tincture of the root is still used today to speed the responses of white cells in fighting infection. It may aid in reducing pain, swelling, and inflammation associated with tennis elbow or other injured tendons and ligaments.

Echinacea spp.
Sunflower Family (Asteraceae)

Dorothy Baird Mattiza

RANGE	1, 2, 3, 4, 5, 7, 8, 9
SIZE	3 feet
BLOOMS	May–July, Perennial

73 · Tansy Aster, Tahoka Daisy

Tansy aster, a showy wildflower in its native western habitat, is widely cultivated. In garden centers, it is sold as Tahoka daisy, a name given it by a commercial seed collector. Growing from a taproot, tansy aster is a many-branched plant, hairy and sticky. Its dense foliage is so finely cut that it has a fernlike appearance. Very narrow red-violet, blue, or purple ray flowers fringe the yellow center disk. Solitary flower heads, two inches across, top the ends of leafy stems. In spite of a similarity in appearance, the *Machaerantheras* are not true asters; they can be identified by a small spine at the tip of each leaf, a characteristic that true asters lack.

Robert & Linda Mitchell

Machaeranthera tanacetifolia (H.B.K.) Nees
Sunflower Family (Asteraceae)

RANGE	7, 8, 9,10
SIZE	4–16 inches
BLOOMS	May–Oct., Annual

74 · Texas Skeleton Plant

Skeleton plant grows upright, with several smooth, slender stems rising from a basal rosette. Upper leaves are reduced to scales, giving the plant its stemmy, skeletal appearance. Solitary flowers are lavender, pale blue, or rose; they are open for only a few morning hours. A slightly cupped, fragrant, two-inch flower head is held in a vase of bracts on the top of each stem. The eight to twelve ray flowers have squared tips, each notched with five tiny, sharp teeth. Easily grown from seed, skeleton plant is particularly attractive massed in the garden. It is found in sandy, clay, or calcareous soils, in openings, and on slopes or prairies. In a habitat with just a little extra moisture, it often forms small, eye-catching colonies. Indians balled droplets of the milky, resinous sap from this plant for chewing gum.

Dorothy Baird Mattiza

Lygodesmia texana (T. & G.) Greene
Sunflower Family (Asteraceae)

RANGE	2, 3, 4, 5, 6, 7, 8, 9, 10
SIZE	2 feet
BLOOMS	Apr.–Oct., Perennial

75 · Western Ironweed

Dorothy Baird Mattiza

Western ironweed is tall and handsome, with one or several stems that rise from underground runners. It forms extensive colonies in roadside ditches, along river bottoms, or in other seasonally moist areas, yet it can also be found along hillsides, prairies, and other dry places. These qualities make it an excellent plant for landscaping. Western ironweed has a broad, flattened inflorescence of many flower heads, closely clustered. Each head is composed of eighteen to twenty-four purple disk florets. Large, alternate leaves have toothed margins and are hairy on the underside. Ironweed is an attractant for butterflies and other pollinators and is an important food source for them.

Vernonia baldwinii Torr.
Sunflower Family (Asteraceae)

RANGE	1, 2, 3, 4, 5, 7, 8, 9
SIZE	2–5 feet
BLOOMS	July–Oct., Perennial

76 · Drummond Skullcap

Scutellaria is a large, worldwide genus. Fourteen of the American species are found in Texas. Drummond skullcap is a low, bushy, hairy little plant. It has the square, four-angled stems characteristic of the mint family. The small, purple to blue flowers are a half-inch long, and two-lipped. The three-lobed lower lip extends tongue-like, well beyond the upper lip. The center lobe is notable for its purple-dotted white spot and notched tip. The small leaves are oval and opposite. Lower leaves are short-stalked; upper leaves are stalkless. Skullcap is a very common plant, found in various soils, in nearly any sunny location. Although skullcaps belong to the mint family, they are bitter and toxic, and should never be used as a flavoring. Their small size, profusion of flowers, and drought tolerance make them an excellent choice for a garden border.

Zoe M. Kirkpatrick

Scutellaria drummondii Benth.
Mint Family (Lamiaceae)

RANGE	1, 2, 3, 4, 5, 6, 7, 8, 9, 10
SIZE	6-12 inches
BLOOMS	Feb.–Nov., Annual/Perennial

From a cluster of basal leaves, this plant produces a single, leafless stalk that bears an umbel of unusual but showy flowers at its tip. Each slender stem in the cluster holds its flower upright when it is young, bends downward as the flower matures, and rises again in fruit. The five petals of the nodding flower are joined only at their base and are bent back, sharply upward. As few as four and as many as 125 flowers have been counted in an umbel. They are magenta, pale-pink, lilac, or white, and have stamens that come together in an unusual cone shape. Broad, tongue-like leaves with smooth margins or indistinct lobes have a central dark red vein, and may be four to twelve inches long. Shooting star is found on open slopes, bluffs bases, in cedar breaks, and in open, moist woods.

Dodecatheon meadia L.
Primrose Family (Primulaceae)

Kay Warmerdam

RANGE	1, 3, 4, 5, 7
SIZE	20 inches
BLOOMS	Mar.–May, Perennial

The noticeable lemon fragrance of this plant led to its botanical and common name. Wherever it blooms, the scent of *Monarda* attracts butterflies and bees. A tea-like beverage can be brewed from the dried leaves or seed heads. The leaves also can contain an oil that is the basis for citronellal, an ingredient used in insect-repellent candles. From its base, lemon beebalm usually has several square, hairy stems. Long-stalked, opposite leaves may reach a length of three inches. They are narrow, with a few teeth on the edges. Numerous white, rosy-pink, or light purple flowers, freckled with dark purple spots, cluster around the stem. Several clusters in series form a spike. *Monarda* often forms large colonies, covering several acres. It is common in pastures, along roadsides, and in other grassy areas.

Monarda citriodora Cerv. ex Lag.
Mint Family (Lamiaceae)

Edith Bettinger

RANGE	1, 2, 3, 4, 5, 6, 7, 8, 9, 10
SIZE	1-3 feet
BLOOMS	Apr.–Oct., Annual/Biennial

79 · Drummond Onion

Vernon L. Wesby

Drummond onion, like all of the *Allium* species, has a characteristic onion odor. Three or more long, slender leaves, about the same length as the hollow stem, rise from the base. Small, white to pink, bell-like flowers are clustered in an umbel at the top of the stem. Fourteen *Allium* species are known in Texas. One of these, the mildly garlic-flavored yellow onion *(A. coryi)*, endemic to the Trans-Pecos, is the only yellow onion native to the United States. All *Allium* species prefer unshaded, grassy areas and form large colonies of plants, flowering in the spring and then again in the fall. A confusing look-alike to the onion group, commonly called crow poison *(Nothoscordum bivalve)*, lacks their distinctive odor. Crow poison has a musky aroma and is not edible.

Allium drummondii Regel
Lily Family (Liliaceae)

RANGE	1, 2, 3, 4, 5, 6, 7, 8, 9, 10
SIZE	1–2 feet
BLOOMS	Mar.–May, Perennial

80 · American Basketflower

American basketflower looks like a thistle but lacks the prickly characteristics of thistles. Each pinkish flower head, composed of disk flowers sitting in a basket-like cup of green bracts, tops the end of a swollen stem. The flowers reach a showy three inches across. The drooping, outer flowers are larger and more brightly colored than the inner, whitish ones. When partially opened, the flowers resemble an old-fashioned shaving brush. Stalkless one- to two-inch leaves, some shallowly toothed, alternate up a grooved or ridged stem. The flowers dry well, or can be useful in fresh arrangements. Their nectar attracts butterflies and other insects.

Centaurea americana Nutt.
Sunflower Family (Asteraceae)

RANGE	1, 2, 3, 4, 5, 6, 7, 8, 10
SIZE	1½ – 5 feet
BLOOMS	May–July, Annual

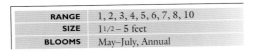

RANGE	1, 2, 3, 4, 5, 7
SIZE	1–4 1/2 feet
BLOOMS	May–Aug., Perennial

A.G. Chaudior

Obedient plant has erect, smooth, square stems. It is found in meadows and swamps, in ditches along highways, and in alluvial soils by streams and rivers. Although obedient plant is not common, it often forms colonies where it does occur, spreading by rhizomes. The sharply lanceolate leaves may be several inches long, narrow, and toothed on the edges. The leaves are opposite; they are stalked near the base but stalkless in the upper sections. Plump, tubular, two-lipped flowers are less than three-fourths of an inch long. The flowers are white, pale lavender-pink, or pink, and the three-lobed lower lip is spotted or streaked with purple lines to guide pollinators inside to the nectar.

Physostegia intermedia (Nutt.) Engelm. & Gray
Mint Family (Lamiaceae)

82 · Gayfeather, Blazingstar

Across Texas, one species or another of *Liatris* will be seen along roadsides in gravelly, sandy, or calcareous soils, on plains, prairies, edges, hillsides, slopes, and roadsides. The stiffly upright plants grow from a corm (an underground bulb-like stem) which may produce a few too many stalks forming a clump. There are no petals, but four to eight disk flowers form flower heads that cluster densely, opening from the top of a terminal spike down-ward. The spikes may be twelve inches in length. Leaves are mostly narrow, and in some species are six inches long near the stem's base. They are crowded and spiral up the stem, becoming progressively smaller until they are small bracts in the flowering spike. Gayfeather has had many medicinal uses, as a diuretic, as a mild kidney or liver tonic, and even as a clinical test for kidney function.

Vernon L. Wesby

Liatris spp.
Sunflower Family (Asteraceae)

RANGE	1, 2, 3, 4, 5, 6, 7, 8, 9, 10
SIZE	1–3 1/2 feet
BLOOMS	Aug.–Oct., Perennial

83 · Prairie Verbena

Laurence Parent

Usually no more than a foot high and often reclining, prairie verbena sometimes paints large areas lavender, pink, bluish, or purple. Plants are hairy, with square stems. Trumpet-shaped with five flattened lobes, the tiny flowers are clustered into half-globes. Opposite, stalked leaves are divided twice into finely cut foliage that adds a lacy background to the rounded flower clusters. Prairie verbena quickly covers barren areas, but it is crowded out as other species invade. It is an important nectar plant for butterflies, blooming throughout the year. It often roots from reclining lower stem joints. Texas has thirty-six species of verbena, many essentially similar.

Verbena bipinnatifida Nutt.
Verbena Family (Verbenaceae)

RANGE	1, 2, 3, 4, 5, 6, 7, 8, 9, 10
SIZE	12–18 inches
BLOOMS	Jan.–Dec., Perennial

84 · Prairie Spiderwort

Tradescantia species are in the same family as dayflowers. Like dayflowers, spiderworts bloom for one day, usually in the morning, but have three radially symmetric petals, whereas dayflowers are bilaterally symmetric, or have two large petals and one small one. The flowers of spiderworts are usually bluish purple but are sometimes violet, pink, or white. The plant itself is erect to trailing, with succulent stems. Alternate, narrow leaves are a foot or more long and look as though they have been folded lengthwise, sheathing the stem. The top two leaves subtend the flower cluster like bracts. Spiderworts do well in cultivation, preferring a moist, sandy soil. The succulent leaves and stems are edible either raw or cooked, but the roots may be poisonous. The fourteen Texas species hybridize, making them difficult to distinguish.

Vernon L. Wesby

Tradescantia occidentalis (Britt.) Smyth
Dayflower Family (Commelinaceae)

RANGE	1, 2, 3, 4, 5, 6, 7, 8, 9, 10
SIZE	6–36 inches
BLOOMS	Feb.–July, Perennial

85 · Bluebell, Prairie Gentian

Texas has two species of *Eustoma*. Both have paired, smooth, bluish green leaves that clasp the stem. Bluebells (*E. grarndiflorum*) and catchfly (*E. exaltatum*) are difficult to distinguish. Flowers are cup-shaped, with five to seven blue to deep blue-violet petals, although the color can vary from pinkish to light blue or white. A dark, purple blotch surrounded by a light halo is centered in the cup, as is a prominent two-lobed yellow stigma. Flowers are two to four inches across. These handsome plants are available in nurseries. They were first cultivated by the Japanese, who recognized their horticultural merit more than forty years ago. Bluebells prefer seasonally moist areas where rainwater sometimes stands, such as roadside ditches, meadows, or prairie swales. Sometimes a single plant or only a few are seen at one location; in other places, bluebells may blanket many acres.

Betty Allison Cawlfield

Eustoma grandiflorum (Raf.) Shinners
Gentian Family (Gentianaceae)

RANGE	1, 2, 3, 4, 5, 6, 7, 8, 9, 10
SIZE	1–2 feet
BLOOMS	June–Sept., Annual/Biennial

86 · Silverleaf Nightshade

The stems and leaves of this prickly plant are covered with tiny stellate, or star-shaped, hairs that give it a silvery-green or gray-green appearance. Leaves are one and one-half to six inches long, with shallowly wavy edges. The five petals of the blue to purple flowers unite at the base for about half their length, then separate into five wide lobes. They look a little like fat, one-inch stars. Flowers are centered with very conspicuous, erect, yellow anthers. Farmers consider silverleaf nightshade a problem plant. The wildflower enthusiast, however, can appreciate the beauty of the blue and silver plants growing in masses along roads, in pastures, and abandoned places. This relative of the tomato is highly toxic to livestock and humans. Its fruit, a half-inch yellow berry, is sometimes used as a substitute for rennet in making cheese.

Zoe M. Kirkpatrick

Solanum eleagnifolium Cav.
Nightshade Family (Solanaceae)

RANGE	1, 2, 3, 4, 5, 6, 7, 8, 9, 10
SIZE	1–3 feet
BLOOMS	Mar.–Oct., Perennial

87 · Baby Blue-Eyes

Betty Allison Cawlfield

Baby blue-eyes is a hairy plant that may be upright or straggling. Its stout stems have many branches. Blue or light purple flowers are one-half to one inch across, with a splash of white in the center. All five petals are notched at the tip, and may be either slightly cupped or wide-open and flat. The deeply cut leaves are divided into five to eleven irregularly lobed segments. Typically, baby blue-eyes is found in moist, shady places such as woodlands or bottomlands, at the edges of thickets, or in brushland. It is often found in masses, carpeting a large area with solid blue.

Nemophila phacelioides Nutt.
Waterleaf Family (Hydrophyllaceae)

RANGE	1, 2, 3, 4, 6, 7
SIZE	28 inches
BLOOMS	Mar.–May, Annual

88 · Blue Star

Amsonia is stiffly upright, with dark green, shiny foliage setting off the inflorescence. Blue, pale blue, or white star-shaped flowers are loosely clustered at the top of each stem, often barely surpassing the alternate leaves. Normally, blue star grows in a moist environment, often in marshes, ditches, bogs, or floodplains. It is recommended for use in the garden where it thrives with a little extra water, but *A. ciliata*, a western species of this lovely plant, lives in drought-prone habitats growing on limestone and chalky hills in Regions 4, 5, 7, and 8.

Amsonia spp.
Dogbane Famiily (Apocynaceae)

Robert & Linda Mitchell

RANGE	1, 2, 3, 4, 5, 6, 7, 8, 9, 10
SIZE	1–4 feet
BLOOMS	Apr.–Nov., Perennial

Phacelia, an American genus of more than two hundred species, is represented in Texas by only twelve species. Like the one pictured, all have coiled, false racemes that uncurl as the flowers open. *Phacelia congesta* is a sticky, hairy plant with an erect, brittle stem. Alternate leaves may be as much as four inches long, deeply cut and divided, and irregularly toothed or lobed. Flowers may be blue, purplish, or white. The flowers are cupped, deeply five-lobed, and only one-fourth of an inch across. Five conspicuous, yellow-tipped stamens protrude from the flower, giving it a whiskered look. Blue curls can be found on all soil types. *Phacelia* is especially adapted to relatively moist habitats such as edges of woods and along streams.

Vernon L. Wesby

RANGE	2, 4, 5, 6, 7, 8, 9, 10
SIZE	1–3 feet
BLOOMS	Mar.–June, Annual/Biennial

Phacelia congesta Hook.
Waterleaf Family (Hydrophyllaceae)

There are more than two hundred species of iris in the Northern Hemisphere, and most of these are in Asia. The five native Texas species occur in bogs and marshes. The Southwest has only a few species of native iris, found primarily in northeast Texas and along the Gulf Coast. Blue flag (*I. virginica*) is an upright to sprawling plant from a stout, creeping rhizome that sometimes forms extensive colonies. Fragrant flowers have three petal-like tepals, or "falls," which droop downward, and three erect inner tepals called "standards." Leaves are alternate, but mostly basal, and sheath the stem. They may reach thirty inches in length but are only slightly more than an inch wide. Indians believed iris root inserted in a tooth cavity would kill the nerve, making the tooth come out. Tea of the boiled root was drunk as a cure for venereal disease.

Vernon L. Wesby

Iris spp.
Iris Family (Iridaceae)

RANGE	1, 2, 3
SIZE	3 feet
BLOOMS	Apr.–May, Perennial

91 · Wild Petunia, Low Ruellia

Edith Bettinger

As the name *humilis* implies, wild petunia is usually a small plant. Conspicuously hairy, it is upright to sprawling, with several square stems forming a clump. Its flowers have five lobes and are two inches or more long. The lavender to light bluish purple trumpets have red or dark purple lines in the throat. Flowers grow singly, or a few at a time, in the axils of leaves. They open in the morning and last only one day. Opposite leaves are crowded, elliptic or ovate, and up to two inches long. Low ruellia grows in full sun or part shade, in dry sandy or clayey soils. It is attractive in wildflower plantings. The many species of wild petunia in Texas are similar but vary in color. Also similar in appearance, cultivated petunias are actually in another family, *Solanaceae*, genus *Petunia*.

Ruellia humilis Nutt.
Acanthus Family (Acanthaceae)

RANGE	1, 2, 3, 4, 5, 7, 8, 9
SIZE	8–30 inches
BLOOMS	Apr.–Oct., Perennial

92 · Missouri Violet

Vernon L. Wesby

Members of the violet family are not hard to identify as a group. Common features are a flat, lower petal that frequently is lined to attract and direct insects to the nectar; two side petals; and two upper petals. Identification by species is almost impossible, however, as they hybridize freely in nature. Missouri violet has the largest range of the nineteen Texas species and is the one most likely to be seen. Flower color varies from pale to dark blue. Twenty to thirty leaves spread from a single crown. They are long-stalked and somewhat heart-shaped. Missouri violet is usually found growing in forested or riparian woodland areas, in partial shade. Most other species found in the state are restricted to east Texas.

Viola missouriensis Greene
Violet Family (Violaceae)

RANGE	1, 2, 3, 4, 5, 7, 8, 10
SIZE	3–10 inches
BLOOMS	Feb.–Apr., Perennial

93 · Herbertia

This charming miniature iris grows in lawns and other grassy places where it is often hidden unless the grass is short. Delicate blossoms of *Herbertia* open each morning and close by mid-afternoon. *Herbertia* is restricted to eastern and coastal parts of Texas. Even there, it is not often seen, but it can occasionally be found in abundance, forming a sheet of blue for a few hours each day. Its dainty, two-inch flowers are formed by six tepals. The three outer tepals are wide-spreading, pale to deep violet, and whitish near the base, with violet spots bordered with purple. Inner tepals are much smaller, dark purple at the base, and pale violet at the tip.

Herbertia lahue (Mol.) Goldblatt
Iris Family (Iridaceae)

RANGE	1, 2, 3, 4, 5
SIZE	12 inches
BLOOMS	Apr.–Oct., Perennial

Betty Allison Cawlfield

94 · Dayflower

Dayflower is first erect, then trailing, occasionally reaching three feet. There are a number of species in Texas similar enough to be difficult to distinguish. All have three petals, the upper two of which can range from white to, more commonly, a beautiful, clear blue. Below these is a third, insignificant, whitish petal that may or may not be noticed. Several buds are clustered in a boat-shaped, sheathing bract, forming a spathe, from which the flower stalks emerge. Squeezing the spathe gently will produce a tear-like drop of liquid, suggesting another common name, widow's tears. The base of the long, linear leaves wraps the succulent stem in a sheath. Dayflowers close early in the day. Edible stems, leaves, and flowers of tender young plants have a pleasant flavor used raw, stewed, or sautéed.

Commelina erecta L.
Dayflower Family (Commelinaceae)

Zoe M. Kirkpatrick

RANGE	1, 2, 3, 4, 5, 6, 7, 8, 9, 10
SIZE	6–18 inches
BLOOMS	May–Oct., Perennial

95 · Blue-Eyed Grass

A.G. Chaudior

Blue-eyed grass, of course, is not grass, nor are all species of *Sisyrinchium* blue, for their flowers range from white, yellow, mauve, and scarlet to purple-rose. The common name is not very appropriate. Members of this genus overlap in range and hybridize, making species difficult to distinguish, but all have dime-sized flowers. The six petals are usually tipped with a small point, and nearly all have a yellow center, or "eve." Flowers emerge from paired bracts that form a spathe. Stems of most species are flat or winged, resembling the grass-like leaves. Alternate leaves are basal, and sheath the stem. Blue-eyed grass sometimes blankets large areas, each clump forming a little blue nosegay.

Sisyrinchium spp.
Iris Family (Iridaceae)

RANGE	1, 2, 3, 4, 5, 6, 7, 8, 9, 10
SIZE	6–20 inches
BLOOMS	Mar.–July, Annual/Perennial

96 · Hairy Hydrolea

The sturdy hydrolea plant is spiny and covered with rough hairs. Several stems may grow from the base, branching in the upper portion. The many flowers are light or dark blue, or purple, an inch across, and very deeply cut into five petal-like lobes. Conspicuous purple stamens are tipped with golden anthers. The flowers are arranged in clusters in the leaf axils and stem ends. Leaves, one to two and one-half inches long and an inch wide, are alternate, some with no stalks. The leaves of *H. ovata* are unique among plants in the waterleaf family because they are not divided or lobed. On the stem, just beneath each leaf, is a prominent spine. Hairy hydrolea forms large colonies, spreading from thick roots in marshy or wet areas around lakes and ponds, and in ditches and seeps.

Hydrolea ovata Choisy
Waterleaf Family (Hydrophyllaceae)

RANGE	1, 2, 3
SIZE	3 feet
BLOOMS	Sept.–Oct., Perennial

Margaret "Peggy" Carey Baily

Larkspur is easily distinguished by the "spur" that extends back from the base of the upper sepal, presumably the lark's spur. The other four sepals have the usual petal form. Larkspur's color can range from white through all shades of blue to blue-violet. Flowers, few to several, open upward along the solitary stem, forming an inflorescence several inches long. The annual larkspur of gardens, *D. ajacis*, has escaped cultivation and is often found growing wild, but it is not a native wildflower. Leaves of larkspur are alternate, deeply palmate-lobed, and one to two inches wide. A tincture of larkspur was an old-fashioned but reliable standby to kill body lice but can cause a rash. This is not surprising; all parts of the plant are poisonous.

Delphinium carolinianum Walt.
Buttercup Family (Ranunculaceae)

RANGE	1, 2, 3, 4, 5, 6, 7, 10
SIZE	1–3 feet
BLOOMS	Apr.–June, Perennial

Slender, delicate, and attractive, celestials are blue with a white eye. Flowers are usually borne in pairs (*gemini*, twin; *flora*, flower) from the tip of the stem. They are more than two inches across and open for only a few hours in the afternoon, so they are often overlooked. The folded leaves have a "W" shape in cross section. They are four to sixteen inches long and less than a half-inch wide, with one leaf taller than the flower. Celestials are found in grassy areas, and in calcareous soil, often in colonies. Their appearance is thought to be dependent upon spring rainfall.

Nemastylis geminiflora Nutt.
Iris Family (Iridaceae)

Jeffery G. Schultz

RANGE	1, 2, 3, 4, 5, 6, 7, 8
SIZE	1 1/2 feet
BLOOMS	Mar.–May, Perennial

99 · Mealy Blue Sage

Andy Wasowski

Mealy blue sage is named for the white feltlike or sometimes purplish, hairy, or farinaceous appearance of the calyx. Its blue flowers are arranged intermittently in dense whorls up a leafless, terminal spike. Opposite leaves are one to three inches in length, have margins that are wavy or coarsely toothed, and have long stalks. The aromatic plants are leafy, especially in the lower portion. Several square stems rise from the base, forming a clump. Mealy blue sage is widespread on limestone soils. Because it flowers for an exceptionally long time and is not readily browsed, it is of great value to pollinators. It is a favorite plant for xeric gardens, and is often available in nurseries.

Salvia farinacea Benth.
Mint Family (Lamiaceae)

RANGE	2, 3, 4, 5, 6, 7, 8, 10
SIZE	6–36 inches
BLOOMS	Mar.–Nov., Perennial

100 · Texas Bluebonnet

Sandyland bluebonnet (*L. subcarnosus*), perhaps misidentified at the time, was adopted in 1901 as the official state flower, but in 1971 it was decided to make all bluebonnets naturally occurring in Texas the state flower. Bluebonnets are identified by their palmately divided, or hand-shaped, leaves and pea-type flowers, closely clustered in an elongated inflorescence, or raceme, at the tips of stems. The petals are blue or purple, and occasionally pink or white. Texas bluebonnet (pictured) and sandyland bluebonnet are the only two species restricted to Texas, with Texas bluebonnet the most widespread. Sandyland bluebonnet is more likely to be seen in the eastern part of the state. In far west Texas, the Big Bend bluebonnet (*L. havardii*) makes a stunning display in the early spring of favorable years.

Lupinus texensis Hook.
Legume Family (Fabaceae)

RANGE	1, 2, 3, 4, 5, 6, 7
SIZE	6–24 inches
BLOOMS	Mar.–May, Annual

GLOSSARY

alkaline: soil with a high exchangeable sodium content.

alluvial: composed of clay, silt, sand, gravel, or similar material deposited by running water.

alternate: placed singly up the stem (not opposite or whorled)

anther: the tip of the stamen, holding the pollen.

axil: the juncture of a leaf or flower with a stalk.

basal: leaves located at the base of the main stem.

blade: expanded portion of a leaf or petal.

bract: a modified leaf subtending a flower.

calcareous: Soil high in calcium carbonate, limestone.

caliche: a crust of calcium carbonate that forms on the stony soil of arid regions.

calyx: the outer whorl of flower parts, usually green.

clasping: partly or wholly surrounding the stem.

cleistogamous: small, non-opening, self-fertilizing flowers.

compound: a leaf completely separated into two or more leaflets.

corm: a short, fleshy underground stem.

cut: sharply incised.

disk flower: the small tubular flower found on the central disk of a composite-type flower head.

endemic: confined to a given region.

farinaceous: containing or rich in starch.

filament: threadlike stalk supporting the anther.

flower head: a dense cluster of flowers on a receptacle.

funnel shape: tubular at the base, flaring upward.

herb: usually non-woody, dies back each year.

incised: cut, often deeply.

inflorescense: a flower cluster or flower head.

lanceolate: long, narrow, tapering toward the tip.

leaflet: a leaf separated completely into two or more parts, appearing as a small leaf.

limestone: sedimentary rock, primarily of calcite.

linear: long, narrow, uniform width, grass-like.

loamy: containing clay, silt, and sand.

lobe: leaf—a rounded margin projection. flower—a petal-like division of a flower tube.

midrib: central vein or rib of a leaf.

opposite: in pairs on opposite sides of the stem.

palmate: divided, three or more fingers spread.

panicle: a branched raceme.

petiole: the leaf stalk.

pinnacle: leaflets on each side of a petiole forming a compound leaf.

pistil: female flower parts (ovary, style, and stigma).

pollen: male spores borne by the anther.

pubescent: covered with hairs.

raceme: a spike-like inflorescence bearing evenly short-stalked flowers.

ray flowers: the outer, petal-like flowers often surrounding the disk of the sunflower family.

resin: sticky liquid produced by some plants.

rhizome: an underground stem or rootstock.

rosette: a cluster of leaves radiating from the stem, at or near the ground.

scape: a naked flower stem rising from the ground.

scarp: a line of cliffs produced by faulting or erosion.

sepals: a leaf-like segment of the calyx.

sessile: attached without a stalk.

sheath: a leaf base completely enclosing the stem.

spathe: a bract that encloses a flower or flower cluster.

spike: stalkless flowers opening up a long, central unbranched stem.

spp: abbreviation for plural of "species. "

sprawling: leaning over, lax.

spreading: parting toward a somewhat flat position.

spur: a tubular extension of a sepal or petal.

stalk: any kind of stem.

stamens: male pollen-bearing reproductive structure, filaments and anthers collectively.

stem: the main stalk of a plant arising from the roots.

swale: a low-lying, wet stretch of land.

subtend: to be below and close to.

taproot: a primary root from which small lateral roots grow.

teeth: small notches of the leaf margin.

tepals: used in the plural for sepals and petals of similar form and not readily differentiated.

terminal: at the tip.

throat: opening of the corolla where petals are fused.

trumpet-shaped: tubular base flaring abruptly.

tube, tubular: hollow, nearly uniform in width, longer than wide.

two-lipped: an upper and lower flower division of an irregular calyx or corolla.

umbel: an often flat-topped inflorescence with stems rising from a common point.

urn-shaped: enlarged at the base, contracted at the throat, without a prominent rim.

whorl: three or more leaves, bracts, or flowers arranged in a circle around a stem.

wing: a ribbon-like membrane along stem or seed edges.

xeric: arid conditions, implying minimal water supply.

VISUAL GLOSSARY

LEAF ARRANGEMENT

ALTERNATE

OPPOSITE

COMPOUND

PINNATE

BASAL WHORL

LEAF FORMS

TOOTHED

OVATE

ELLIPTICAL

LANCEOLATE

LINEAR

INCISED

FLOWER ARRANGEMENT

UMBEL

PANICLE

RACEME

SPIKE

COMPOSITE

FLOWER FORMS

TWO-LIPPED

FUNNEL

PEA

TRUMPET

BELL

TUBULAR

FURTHER READING

Similarities among many species make them difficult to identify. Even experts have problems. If you want to know more, the Native Plant Society of Texas highly recommends the following books. These books are the primary source for plant names, descriptions, locations, uses and other information used in this book.

Ajilvsgi, Geyata. *Wildflowers of the Big Thicket, East Texas, and Western Louisiana*. College Station, TX: A & M University Press, 1979.

Butterfly Gardening for the South. Dallas, TX: Taylor Publishing Co., 1990.

Correll, Donovan Stewart, and Marshall Conring Johnston. *Manual of the Vascular Plants of Texas*. Vol . 6, of contributions from Texas Research Foundation: A Series of Botanical Studies, edited by Cyrus Longworth Lundell. Richardson, TX: Texas Research Foundation, 1970.

Enquist, Marshall. *Wildflowers of the Texas Hill Country*. Austin, TX: Lone Star Botanical, 1987.

Ham, Hal. *South Texas Wildflowers Collection One*. Kingsville, TX: Conner Museum, Texas A & I University, 1984.

Harrington, H. D. *Western Edible Wild Plants*. Albuquerque, NM: The University of New Mexico Press, 1967.

Hatch, Stephan L., Kancheepuram N. Gandhi, and Larry E. Brown. *Checklist of the Vascular Plants of Texas*. College Station, TX: Texas A & M University, 1990.

Jones, Fred B. *Flora of the Texas Coastal Bend*, Third Edition. Sinton, TX: Welder Wildlife Foundation, 1982.

Kindscher, Kelly. *Edible Wild Plants of the Prairie, An Ethnobotanical Guide*. Lawrence, TX: University Press of Kansas, 1987.

Kirkpatrick, Zoe Merriman. *Wildflowers of the Western Plains*. Austin, TX: University of Texas Press, 1992 .

Loughmiller, Campbell, and Lynn Loughmiller. *A Field Guide, Texas Wildflowers*. Austin, TX: University of Texas Press, 1984.

Medicinal Plants of the Mountain West. Santa Fe, NM: Museum of New Mexico Press, 1979.

Moore, Michael. *Medicinal Plants of the Desert and Canyon West*. Santa Fe, MN: Museum of New Mexico Press, 1989.

Rickett, Harold William. *Wild Flowers of the United States*. Volume 3, parts one and two. New York: McGraw-Hill Book Co., 1969.

Rose, Francis L., and Russell W. Standtmann. *Wildflowers of the Llano Estacado*. Dallas, TX: Taylor Publishing Co., 1986.

Rowell, Chester M. *A Guide to the Identification of Plants Poisonous to Livestock of Western Texas.* San Angelo, TX: Angelo State University.

Sheldon, Robert A. *Roadside Geology of Texas.* Missoula, MT, 1979.

Tull, Delena. *A Practical Guide to Edible & Useful Plants.* Austin, TX: Texas Monthly Press, 1987.

____, and George Oxford Miller. *A Field Guide to Wildflowers, Trees and Shrubs of Texas.* Houston, TX: Gulf Publishing Company, 1991.

Warnock, Barton H. *Wildflowers of the Big Bend Country.* Alpine, TX: Sul Ross State University, 1970.

Wasowski, Sally, with Andy Wasowski. *Native Texas Plants Landscaping Region by Region.* Austin, TX: Texas Monthly Press, 1988.

Wildflowers of Texas. Bryan, TX: Shearer Publishing, 1985.

Wildflowers of the Davis Mountains and Marathon Basin, Texas. Alpine, TX: Sul Ross State University, 1977.

Wildflowers of the Guadalupe Mountains and the Sand Dune Country, Texas. Alpine, TX: Sul Ross State University, 1974.

INDEX

ACKNOWLEDGMENTS

CO-CHAIRMEN   Kate Hillhouse
Dorothy Baird Mattiza

CONSULTING BOTANISTS   David Creech, Ph.D.
Benny J. Simpson
Chester Rowell, Ph.D.

PLANT LISTS   The Membership of the Native Plant
Society of Texas

PHOTOGRAPHERS   Members of the Native Plant Society of Texas,
Robert and Linda Mitchell, and Laurence Parent

PHOTOGRAPHY EDITING   Marie Wesby
Vernon L. Wesby

JUDGE OF PHOTOGRAPHY   Bob Parvin

EDITING   Melinda Larson
Susan Sander

PROOFING   Elizabeth Ohm
Susan Tracy
Patricia Wilkie

WORD PROCESSING   Charles Wilkie